Theatre Royal
STRATFORD EAST

Aarawak Moon Productions and
Theatre Royal Stratford East present

Shoot 2 Win

by **Tracey Daley**, **Jo Martin**, and **Josephine Melville**

First performed at Theatre Royal Stratford East
on 11 February 2002

Theatre Royal Stratford East
Gerry Raffles Square
Stratford
London E15 1BN
www.stratfordeast.com

Shoot 2 Win

by **Tracey Daley, Jo Martin** and **Josephine Melville**

Sandra	Maxine Burth
Mandy	Lorna Brown
Jackie	Karen Bryson
Shenequa	Nadine Marshall
Beverly	Susan Salmon
Carrie	Yaa
Zowie	Juliet Prew

Director	Paulette Randall
Designer	Ellen Cairns
Lighting Designer	Paul Anderson
Sound Designer	Ceri Nicholls

Theatre Royal Stratford East from 11 February 2002 to 9 March 2002.

National Tour Spring 2002

March

12 – 16 7.45pm
(Matinees Thurs 14, 1.30pm, Sat 16, 4pm)
The Courtyard, West Yorkshire Playhouse (0113) 213 7700

19 – 23 8pm
Everyman Theatre, Liverpool (0151) 709 4776

April

2 – 6 8pm
Palace Theatre, Westcliff On Sea (01702) 342564

9 – 13 7.30pm
Haymarket Theatre, Leicester (0116) 253 9797

16 – 20 7.45pm
The Wolsey, Ipswich (01473) 295900

25 – 27 8pm
The Gardner Arts Centre, Brighton (01273) 685861

May

7 – 11 8pm
Contact, Manchester (0161) 274 0600

The Company

Lorna Brown Mandy

Lorna is thrilled to be working with Stratford East again having played Princess in Stratford East's community tour musical *One Dance Will Do*. Trained at the Central School of Speech and Drama, Lorna has recently appeared in Talawa's *Anansi Steals The Wind* at Queen Elizabeth Hall and also took part in a script workshop for *Shoot 2 Win* with Aarawak Moon Productions. Other theatre credits include *Othello* (New Vic, Stoke), *Zumbi* (Theatre Royal Stratford East/Tour), *Up Against The Wall* (Tricycle/Tour) and *Once on this Island*, a new musical which transferred from Birmingham Rep to the West End. Film and television credits include *The Bill*, *Casualty*, *Murder Most Horrid* and the award-winning *Bad Girls*. Singer-songwriter Lorna is currently recording her first solo album, and has previously performed with Courtney Pine and Gladys Knight.

Karen Bryson Jackie

Trained at LAMDA, this is Karen's first appearance at Stratford East. Karen's theatre work includes *Flyin' West* at the Orange Tree Theatre, Richmond; *Luminosity, Back To Methuselah, A Comedy Of Errors, La Lupa, The Winter's Tale, Epitaph for the Official Secrets Act* and *The Lion, The Witch and The Wardrobe* for the RSC; *Romeo and Juliet* for Birmingham Rep; *Our Day Out* and *Antigone* for the Wolsey Theatre and *The Name of The Game* for the Wolsey Studio, Ipswich; Lady Macduff in the English Touring Theatre's production of *Macbeth* which toured for several months, finishing at the Lyric Theatre Hammersmith; Janet Welch in *Golden Girls* at Colchester and *Beowulf* for the English Shakespeare Company. Screen work includes the feature film *Maybe Baby*; *Lenny Blue* for Granada; episodes of *Holby City*, *The Bill* and *Grange Hill*; the Channel 4 film *Longest Memory*, a short film called *Through Water*, the new feature film version of *The Changeling*, *Frontiers*, playing the character of Susan, the part of Deemon in the independent film *Diana Delusion* and a short independent film entitled *Zulu-9*.

Maxine Burth Sandra

Maxine trained at Rose Bruford College of Speech and Drama and has worked extensively in theatre, television and radio since. Her theatre credits include: *Wicked Games* and *All The Helicopter Night* (West Yorkshire Playhouse); *Handicap Race* (Salisbury Playhouse); *A Raisin In The Sun* (Black Arts, Green Room); *Stamping, Shouting, Singin Home* (Northampton Theatre Royal) and *Translations* (London Half Moon). For television Maxine has appeared in: *Always and Everyone*, *Wilmot*, *Coronation Street*, *Big Meg Little Meg*, *Medics* and *Band of Gold* (Granada); *Emmerdale* and *Lost For Words* (Yorkshire); *Own Goal* (Pagoda Film & Television); *Liverpool One* (Lime Street Productions); *The Bill* (Thames); *Hetty Wainthrop Investigates*, *Out Of The Blue* and *Cardiac Arrest* (BBC). Her most recent television appearance was in *Playing The Field* (Tiger Aspect). On film Maxine has appeared in the Granada Film Productions *Girls Night* and *Heart*; she played the lead role in *Eulogy* (Frigid Films) as well as working on *Kisko – A Life For A Life* (Film Europe Ltd) and *Deadly Voyage* (BBC/HBO/Viva Pictures). Maxine has also worked extensively in Radio Drama.

Nadine Marshall Shenequa

Trained at the Rose Bruford College of Speech and Drama, this is Nadine's first appearance at Stratford East. Her most recent theatre appearance was the lead in *The Last Valentine* at the Almeida. Other theatre credits include: *Oroonoko*, *Timon Of Athens*, *Henry VIII*, *Camino Real* and *Spanish Tragedy* (all RSC); *The Shining* (Royal Court); *Kids*; *Lysistrata, Medea, Three Sisters, Stamping, Shouting and Singing Home* (Rose Bruford). Nadine has also just completed work on two BBC Radio productions, *Scars* and *Freefall*, prior to which she took part in a rehearsed reading of *The Homelife of Polar Bears* at the Royal Court. Recent film and television work includes *Club Le Monde* and *Family Affairs*.

Juliet Prew Zowie

This is Juliet's first time at Theatre Royal and she is delighted to be here. Recent theatre credits include;

Get Up And Tie Your Fingers (NTC); *The Reader* (Citizens Theatre, Glasgow); *Speaking In Tongues* (Hampstead Theatre); *We All Fall Down* (Immediate Theatre, Hackney); *Cinderella* (Derby Playhouse); *All My Sons* and a one-woman show, *A Place In The Desert* (Bristol Old Vic); *Here Is Monster, The Golden Age* (Show Of Strength, Bristol) and *Normal: The Düsseldorf Ripper* (Finborough). For television; *Casualty* and a P.D.James murder mystery, *A Mind To Murder*. Juliet is a regular voice for BBC Radio Drama and short stories, BBC 2's *Wild* and to her undying amusement, has been the voice for *The Phone Bar/Singles Bar* advertisements. She is a long-standing member of the a cappella group *Smashing Dishes*.

Susan Salmon Beverly

This is Susan's second visit to Stratford East having previously appeared in *Party Girls*. Trained at RADA her recent theatre credits include *Office* (Soho Theatre) and Helena in *A Midsummer Nights Dream* (RNT Tour). Other theatre includes *Arms And The Man* (Orange Tree Theatre). Susan's film and television credits include; *Grange Hill, EastEnders* (BBC) and *On The Edge* (directed by Newton Aduaka).

Yaa Carrie

Trained at the Arts Educational School, Yaa recently made her Stratford East debut in the pantomime *Aladdin*. Yaa has appeared in many musical theatre productions including Sarafina in *The Lion King* (Lyceum Theatre), Simon Callow's production of *Carmen Jones* (Old Vic), *Fame* (Cambridge Theatre), *Cats* (Hamburg) and the original UK tour of *42nd Street*. Other theatre and dance credits include *A Midsummer Nights Dream* (Crucible/ National Theatre Athens), *Push* (Young Vic), Jonzi D's *Aeroplane Man* and *Sisters In Jazz* (Sadlers Wells). Television credits include *Top Of The Pops, Smash Hits Awards, Olivier Awards* and *The South Bank Show: The Making Of The Lion King*. Yaa has also modelled for Coca-Cola/Schweppes, Levis and Ebony and Vogue magazines. In between all of this, she has also managed to find time to provide lead and backing vocals for Ben Onono and Noel McKoy, choreographed her first musical *Passports To The Promised Land* and various fashion and trade shows!

Production

Tracey Daley Writer

Tracey began singing at an early age and has attended the Wolfall School of Operatic Arts in New York. She has released many singles, one of which was included on the compilation *British Soul Hits 1*. Under the name of Trichelle she has supported many artists in the UK, USA and the Carribean. She has also performed at Theatre Royal Stratford East as a guest artiste for *The Posse*. A keen artist, she designs and makes hand-made afrocentric style greeting cards. Her artistic flair has lead to great input into the designs of Aarawak Moon merchandise, flyers and programmes. Tracey is a mother of two.

Jo Martin Writer

Jo became a member of the Theatre Royal Stratford East Youth Theatre and her first professional job was at Stratford East where Philip Hedley gave her her Equity card! Jo has been working in television, radio and theatre for the past fifteen years. Her acting credits include *The Real McCoy* for BBC2, Lenny Henry's *Chef* for BBC1 and *The Murder of Stephen Lawrence* for Granada. Jo has recently finished filming *Always And Everyone* for Carlton Television, and can also be seen in the current series of *Casualty*. Her extensive theatre credits include *Pecong* and *Victor And The Ladies* (Tricycle Theatre) and a fifteen month run with the Royal Shakespeare Company where she appeared in *Oroonoko* and *Don Carlos*, which at the end of the run at Stratford-upon-Avon, went to the U.S.A. Jo is also an accomplished director and writer. A resident performer and writer for *Club Class* (Channel 5), she has also written for various television and radio programmes including two series of the comedy show *The Airport* for Radio 4, which was nominated for an award. Jo recently received the Best Actress award at the BFI Black Film Festival 2001, for *Dead Meat* (directed by Don Letts).

Josephine Melville Writer

Josephine has appeared in several productions at Theatre Royal Stratford East, including *Moon Over A Rainbow Shawl*, *Party Girls*, *Red Riding Hood*, *Dick Whittington* (at Greenwich Theatre), *Blaggers* and *The BiBi Crew* shows. She began her career as a dancer and has toured in places such as Egypt, Bahrain and Dubai. She crossed over into acting of which her many theatre credits include *Hair* (Theatre Clywd), *O Babylon* and *Unfinished Business* (Talawa Theatre Company), *Godspell* (Oldham, Manchester) and *Meetings* (Nitro, formerly The Black Theatre Co-Op). Josephine also toured for two years across the USA in *Macbeth* (Committed Artists of Great Britain). As a founder member and director of *The BiBi Crew*, Josephine wrote, performed and produced comedy shows that were staged in London and toured nationally, as well as being invited to perform at the festival in the B.A.M. Majestic Theatre in New York. Josephine's television credits include *Eastenders* for BBC1, *The Bill* for LWT and *Prime Suspect* for Granada Television. Her writing credits include a children's play for Carib Theatre Company as well as her work as co-writer for all *BiBi Crew* material, two series of *The Airport* for Radio 4 and *Club Class* for Channel 5.

Paulette Randall Director

Paulette has a long association with Stratford East and has directed many shows here including *Funny Black Women On The Edge*, *Blaggers* and almost all of *The Posse* shows. In 1999/2000, Paulette took part in Stratford East's New Musicals Development Project. Paulette is an Associate Director of the Tricycle Theatre for whom she has directed *Pinchy Kobi And The Seven Duppies*, *Pecong* and August Wilson's *Two Trains Running*. Other theatre credits include: *Sanctuary* (Joint Stock); *Temporary Rupture* (Black Theatre Co-Op and Croydon Warehouse); *For Coloured Girls Who Considered Suicide When The Rainbow Is Enuf* (BAC, Albany Empire); *The Amen Corner* (Bristol Old Vic) and *Leave Taking* (National Theatre). She has also directed two half-hour sitcom scripts in the Channel 4 Sitcom Festival 1997, and one called *All Talk* by Paul McKenzie for the 1998 festival. In 2001, Paulette directed Richard Blackwood's one-man theatre show, which went on an extensive tour. In the same year, she also directed a pilot episode for a black women's sketch show for Chrysalis Entertainment. Paulette has considerable television producing experience, including *Desmond's*, *The Real McCoy*, *Porkpie*, *Marvin* (pilot) and *Coming Atcha* starring Cleopatra (Initial for Channel 4). She has also worked for Carlton TV as the Development Producer, and appeared in the pilot of the cultural magazine show *Live Lyrics*.

Ellen Cairns Designer

Ellen trained at Glasgow School of Art and The Slade in London. She won the Arts Council theatre design bursary in 1981, and subsequently became resident designer at Liverpool Playhouse for three years, and then the Half Moon Theatre in London. Designs include *Moon On A Rainbow Shawl* at The Almeida; *Two Trains Running* at The Tricycle and *Amen Corner* at Bristol Old Vic, both directed by Paulette Randall. Seventeen productions for Talawa Theatre, directed by Yvonne Brewster, including *The Gods Are Not To Blame* at Riverside Studios, *King Lear* at The Cochrane Theatre, and *One Love* at The Lyric, Hammersmith. West End credits include *Trafford Tanzi,* and *Fences*. She works extensively abroad and recent openings include *Les Miserables* at a 4,000 seat venue in Estonia, and *Darkness At Noon,* based on Arthur Koestler's novel, in Stockholm.

Paul Anderson Lighting Designer

Paul returns to Theatre Royal Stratford East having recently worked on the pantomime *Aladdin*. Paul trained at Mountview Theatre School and York College of Arts and Technology. For Complicite: *Light, The Noise Of Time, Mnemonic* (Drama Desk award and Lucille Lortell award), *The Chairs* (nominated for Tony, Drama Desk and Olivier awards). Relights for *The Street of Crocodiles, The Caucasian Chalk Circle* and *The Three Lives of Lucie Cabrol*. Other design: *A Servant to Two Masters* (Royal Shakespeare Company and West End); *As I Lay Dying, Twelfth Night, West Side Story, Guys and Dolls* and *Arabian Nights* (Young Vic); *The Threesome, Pinnochio* (Lyric Hammersmith); *Special Occasions, Hospitality, A coupla white chicks sitting around talking* and *Blue Window* (North America Theatre UK); *The Double Bass* (Man in the Moon); *The Christie Brown Exhibition* (Wapping Hydraulic Power Station); *Cinderella* (Theatre Royal Stratford East) and *Rediscovering Pompeii* at the Academia Italiana (IBM Exhibition).

Aarawak Moon Productions

Aarawak Moon Productions is a black, all-female company formed in November 1997 by Tracey Daley, Jo Martin and Josephine Melville. Set up to provide live entertainment and cultural experience to the black community in venues such as comedy clubs and theatres, Aarawak Moon aims to make diverse cultural entertainment accessible to audiences around the U.K., striving towards mainstream entertainment from a black perspective.

Special thanks to

Adidas, All England Netball Association, *Ann Summers – Fashion and Passion retailer – website: annsummers.com*, Black Beauty and Hair, Black Hair Magazine, *Boots the Chemist*, Herbal Smoking Mixture provided by Honeyrose Products Ltd., Holland and Barrett, *Impact Office Furniture*, Newham Sports Development, Palmers Skincare and Haircare Products, Paperchase Products Ltd., Pride Magazine, Prop Portfolio Ltd., Puma UK, Reebok, Slim·fast Foods Ltd., Smirnoff, *Tommy Hilfiger*, Twinings.

Shoot 2 Win

In conversation with James Peries (New Writing Manager at Theatre Royal Stratford East), the writers of *Shoot 2 Win*, Tracey Daley, Jo Martin, and Josephine Melville discuss the play, the writing process, their long standing relationship with Theatre Royal Stratford East, and their own production company Aarawak Moon. (James Peries – JP; Tracey Daley – TD; Jo Martin – JM; Josephine Melville – JME.)

JP   How did the play's netball setting come about?

JM   We were looking for somewhere to place seven strong female characters. When Philip Hedley (Artistic Director at Theatre Royal Stratford East) commissioned us, he said he wanted us to create a piece for five strong black actresses. So we spent a long time thinking about where we could put five women to tell their stories, and then one day Jo said 'Netball' and we all said 'yes', we knew that was the one. For a netball team, the five characters became seven.

JP   Did you all play netball?

JM   Oh yes, and the play is all about the idea of a team. The characters don't work as a team and they need to come together. There's one method of play in Netball called Zone Defence and you need to be a really strong team to play it, because you're not working 'man on man' but only in your zone, and that has to connect with the other zones of your team mates.

TD   There's a piece of us all in all of the characters. Some of the characters are based on people we know, but there are also elements of us as well.

JP   How do three people write a play together? It's quite unusual.

JM   It's not easy; it could easily have crashed. We sat down and talked about the characters for days, weeks, and months, developing and seeing the characters.

TD   We did a lot of back work on the history of the characters, from when they were babies up until now, and from now until the end of the play.

JM   When we went off to write separately there was no discrepancy between the way we each viewed the characters. We knew how they each spoke; amongst us we would often say 'That's a Shenequa line, that's a Bev line'.

JP   You are all performers. How much did you get up and act out the way that the characters might be?

JM   We act out everything, every minute we're getting up. In our readings you could literally see them and breathe them.

JP How did being performers influence the opportunities you created for other performers who would play these roles?

JM We started writing thinking that we were going to be in it. But in the process of doing it, the writing became more exciting than the idea of being in it. As an actor and director I think you instinctively know what you have to give a performer. The experience of being in the rehearsal room watching other performers bringing your characters to life – and inspiring rewrites – is untouchable.

JP I can see how you could work to agree the characters, and then do some writing separately, but what about the storyline and the whole rhythm of the play?

JM We agreed the story line very clearly. All of the characters' 'back stories' were so interesting we could easily have become sidetracked if we hadn't fixed that in our minds early on.

JP The play is set in one location over the course of a day, what did that give you in the writing?

JM It gives the audience a sense of the momentum building, and the sense that the netball tournament, and the tensions within the team are leading towards some inevitable climax. Also, the audience share most of the same experience and information with the characters; and they discover the various revelations at the same time as the characters. That was a change; in an early draft one of the biggest revelations was known by the audience from the start, now they find out when the rest of the team do.

JP You've all done a lot of writing before, but not necessarily a play?

TD I'm mainly a songwriter, but I've written short stories and ideas for plays in the past, and I've been writing a novel forever! The great thing about that is that so many things have happened in my life since I started writing it. I've discovered a lot about what is interesting subject matter, what is important in the writing, and how to edit!

JM I began with the youth theatre at Stratford East, and developed lots of skills in improvisation, which would then be written into scripts, and those skills have eventually led towards this play. As an actress I've learnt a lot from plays I've performed in. In the field of comedy I've written for The Real McCoy, Comedy Nation, some sketches for Lenny Henry, and I was involved in a team who wrote three series of a comedy called The Airport for Radio 4.

JME Some time ago I wrote some synopses for television plays that were well received by TV companies, but I didn't want to make the changes they suggested; I had very clear things I wanted to say, and didn't want to trim them. After that I did a lot of work in Youth Theatre and Education work and wrote a Theatre In Education play for Carib Theatre Company which toured in the London area. Then I also worked on The Airport, which was a great experience. Having been an actress it was great to be able to create characters and see them right through to production.

JP   How has creating this play been different from that earlier writing?

JM   We didn't come at this with the intention to write a comedy. We just felt that we had this story to tell, and strong ideas about the characters. It was only at the first read-through that we saw by the reactions of others that there was a lot of comedy within the drama.

JME   If we'd approached it from the idea of it being a comedy we could have fallen into all kinds of traps: being led by gags, or in-jokes between us. In sketch show writing it can be very exciting, you work as a team, and there can be a million ideas going around, but getting into a sketch is easy, getting out of it is very difficult.

JM   If a character says something in this play it has to be character led, it may also be funny, but it has to come from truth rather than a contrived moment. I don't like to call it a comedy, if you're going to say comedy then call it a comedy drama, but we just set out to write a drama.

JP   You all have a history with Theatre Royal Stratford East, what's your involvement been?

JM   I was in the Stratford East Youth Theatre, and then did a part time job there before going to Drama School, and I got my equity card there by playing a role in *El Dorado*, a play by Michael Abbensetts. Then I went off to discover the world, and later they brought me back to Stratford East to direct *The Posse*. *The Posse* was a troupe of eight gorgeous talented black actors that were happening around the early to mid 1990s, they created revue shows, but they would have a narrative storyline running through it. So I got my directing break at Stratford East too, and have done the Directors' Course that Stratford East runs.

TD   I've always been a singer songwriter, and have done gigs in the U.K and U.S and released tracks. Having close friends in the theatre world made me want to bring the two together, and we're always looking at ways to incorporate each other in our projects. I did a guest appearance with the comedy team *The Posse* and that was my first experience of the Theatre Royal Stratford East stage. Many projects have branched off from the people I have met at Stratford East, but Stratford East was the root. In 2001 I took part in the four-week Musical Theatre Writing Workshop held by Stratford East, and that was a great experience. It's inspired me to write a musical which will be one of Aarawak Moon's future projects.

JME   I started off as a dancer, but my first piece at Stratford East was acting in *Moon on a Rainbow Shawl* by Errol John. Then I went off and did a lot of musicals and pop videos.

JM   She's always on MTV! Look out for those old pop videos: she's with Limahl in Kajagoogoo's *Too Shy*, and in Culture Club's *Karma Chameleon* that's Jo doing the Can Can!

JME   That all broadened my horizons, but I was looking to carry on acting, and follow through on the writing side. I was lucky enough to be part of the BiBi Crew which was seven women who wrote and directed their own material. You could say it was another baby of the Theatre Royal, and inspired by *The Posse*.

JP   **From your viewpoint, what has Theatre Royal Stratford East's role been in the developing of new shows and new talent, particularly with black performers?**

JME   The Theatre Royal has created many shows that gather a lot of talents together, and as a black performer you would want to come and see what's going on. People would come along, link up, and you'd really get to know who was on the scene. That was really important because the dearth of black performers on TV wasn't going to give you that knowledge. Because the Theatre Royal was doing those productions, it really was the umbrella for so much that was developed, a great meeting place for black talent. It was very empowering because we were given the space, the protectiveness and support to be creative, to be adventurous, and to get the work on the stage. Also, once a show was over, it was about keeping those channels open with the audience and community, taking work out of London and on to a National tour as we are doing with *Shoot 2 Win* after the London run. *The Posse* and the BiBi Crew also had the opportunity to work internationally. In 1996 we set up our own company – Aarawak Moon Productions – and our comedy improvisation show *Blaggers* was the last show before the Theatre Royal closed for refurbishment. We feel so committed to Stratford East, we were determined to be the first play back in the theatre after re-opening.

JP   **Where does the name 'Aarawak Moon' come from?**

JM   Aarawak is the indigenous population of Jamaica - the Aarawak Indians; they were wiped out, but some of us have got Aarawak blood in us, and we're all Jamaicans. We wanted to highlight their name, put it out there, and we like it.

JME   And Moon? Well, it's a Woman thing, you know?

JP   **How did you come to form Aarawak Moon Productions?**

JM   We didn't set out to have a company. We were always together, very 'high chested' people always looking at things and commenting on things, big big talking, but not as much doing. Then The Comedy Store were looking for a female comedian, and I got the job in the Comedy Store Players. There was no-one black in the audience, just a black bouncer. So we imagined what we could do if we put on a similar night ourselves, and created *Blaggers* as an impro comedy show with two teams of black performers. It was a huge hit, and led to comedy workshops when audience members said they wanted to have a go, and a Y*oung Blaggers* version. As a performer it's such a buzz, it really challenges you, but what you get back from the audience is incredible.

TD We also produce a night called *The Lunar Lounge*; I'd always had this idea of a living room type environment where you could have people going around serving drinks, a live jazz band, poets, comedians, dancers, up-and-coming talent, and a character-led host.

JM We've developed workshops around performance skills, play writing, comedy and improvisation which accompany *Shoot 2 Win* both in London and on tour. So you're not just getting the play itself, but we're working in the communities we visit, and helping the venues to tap into some of their new audiences where sometimes they haven't done before. We want to encourage those new audiences with *Shoot 2 Win*, and really establish that there is a market for black work both in and out of London, and that the relationship with local theatres and visiting companies can have longevity.

JP **What plans do you have for the future?**

TD We'd like to do international festivals, and we see the Blaggers concept touring nationally.

JM We have a musical in mind, and a screenplay of *Shoot 2 Win*. The trick is to run our company, keep all these things bubbling, but still find the space to write new material.

JME And that's to do with getting the funding to allow us to be creative. The Arts Council has enabled us to take this play on tour, and we intend to break through to new audiences with it, and establish a successful black play outside of London. Keeping that momentum going is really important to us, and we're still seeking the funding to keep feeding that audience with vibrant entertainment that they connect with.

Netball: the rules of the game

Goal Shooter

has the main responsibility for shooting the goals and scoring the points! Located in the attacking third of the court (including the goal circle).

Goal Attack

can play in the attacking two thirds of the court. Her task is to ensure the ball moves up into the goal circle and she can also shoot goals.

Wing Attack

is responsible for passing the ball to the shooters, Wing Attack can't enter the goal circle but remains in the attacking two-thirds.

Centre

gets about a bit as Centre can play the entire court except for the goal circles. An all-rounder, the centre is often team captain and supports both the attacking and defensive sides of the team.

Wing Defence

tries hard to get in the way of the opposing side's play to the goal net. The role involves marking the Wing attacker and trying to make sure the ball never makes it into the opposing team's Goal Circle.

Goal Defence

defends the Goal Attacker. She tries to stop the ball making it into the goal circle and is often instrumental in moving play back towards her team's net.

Goal Keeper

keeps tabs on the Goal Shooter – keeping her out of the Goal Circle whenever possible and trying hard to get between the ball and the net.

Particularly popular among women, Netball is something most of us will remember as a part of our school years – along with the stylish PE knicker.

Netball is related to and developed from the game of Basketball which was invented in the USA in 1891. A misunderstanding in the reading of the diagram and instructions for Basketball led to an altered version of the game where players didn't move from their allocated areas of the court.

The game became known as Netball in 1897, and used larger rings and nets instead of baskets. With the first rule book published in 1900, the game became increasingly popular in England and in 1926 the All England Netball Association was founded. Netball officially became an Olympic sport in 1995.

Netball is a team game, with the emphasis on co-operation. Played by two teams of seven players, netball is a fast (and often furious) game that requires many different skills including running, jumping, catching and throwing. The main aim of the game is to score as many goals as you can. Only two players can actually score these goals – the Goal Shooter and the Goal Attacker, and they must score from within a specific area of the court called the Goal Circle – a semi-circle centred on the goal line. Although only the Goal Shooter and Goal Attacker can score the goals, the entire team is responsible for setting up chances and seeing opportunities – with the emphasis of the game on co-operation, the whole team needs to play together to win the game.

For more information about the history of netball, the rules of the game and how to get involved visit the All England Netball Association's website at www.england-netball.co.uk or call the AENA at Netball House, 01462 442 344.

Theatre Royal Stratford East

The Theatre Royal Stratford East became world famous in the fifties and sixties as the home of the Theatre Workshop company, under the direction of Joan Littlewood. Her productions of new shows such as *A Taste Of Honey*, *The Hostage*, and *Oh, What A Lovely War* brought a much-needed robust spirit to British Drama. This tradition of adventurous and occasionally controversial work was maintained at Stratford East throughout the Eighties when the quantity of new work was diminishing elsewhere. The theatre strives to constantly further its reputation for speaking to its diverse local audience. This commitment to portraying, expressing, and giving voice to the large number of social and ethnic community experiences in East London has become one of the Theatre Royal's defining features, and continues into the new millennium. The Theatre Royal believes in a continuous loop between work on the stage, interaction with the audience, and work in the community; all of which then brings new subject matter, new performance styles, and new talents to the Theatre Royal's stage.

Information

Would you like to receive regular information on what's going on at Theatre Royal Stratford East?

If you'd like to hear the latest news about the theatre, our future plans and shows, call the Box Office now on 020 8534 0310 and ask to be added to our mailing list.

Alternatively, log onto our website at www.stratfordeast.com and join via email!

Contacting the Theatre

Theatre Royal Stratford East
Gerry Raffles Square
Stratford
London E15 1BN

Box Office:	020 8534 0310
Administration:	020 8534 7374
Fax:	020 8534 8381
Education Direct line:	020 8279 1108
Press Direct line:	020 8279 1123 or 020 8534 2178
e-mail:	theatreroyal@stratfordeast.com
website:	www.stratfordeast.com

Offices open	Mon – Fri 10am – 6pm
Box Office open	Mon – Fri 10am – 7pm
	Sundays from 5.30pm - (if performances are scheduled)

New Musicals for a New Century

Why are less young people going to the theatre?

Why are the more exciting musical forms that top today's charts not featured in British theatre?

Why is London and the U.K's wonderful mix of races hardly influencing the development of its musical theatre?

The Theatre Royal Stratford East believes the answers to these questions are all connected, and over the last three years it has made considerable strides forward in the development of contemporary musicals using today's music.

The heart of the Theatre Royal's Musical Theatre project has been the full-time month-long Musical Theatre Writing Workshops held every July. The workshops are led by two lecturers, Fred Carl and Robert Lee, who are from the only full-time musical theatre writing course in the world, at the Tisch School of the University of New York.

Each Workshop is attended by up to twenty-five participants, the majority of whom are Black and Asian. The script writers are experienced in theatre, although not usually in musicals. The composers have a track record in popular music but often no experience at all in theatre. To recruit for the workshops much work is done to search out musical talents in basement studios, independent record labels, music training courses, colleges or wherever, and to interest them in the idea of expressing themselves in theatrical forms.

The Workshops are entirely practical, and they lead on to the commissioning of twenty-minute musicals and eventually full-length shows. The highly successful musical *One Dance Will Do* toured East London prior to the re-opening of the Theatre Royal, and was written by the team of Hope Massiah and Delroy Murray, who first collaborated on the July 2000 workshop. They have now been commissioned to write a full-length musical for the Theatre Royal stage. Another musical, *Baiju Bawra*, comes to the Theatre Royal in March 2002, with music by Niraj Chag who took part in the very first July workshop in 1999.

We have set up a parallel process of musical development workshops with teenagers and we have staged, with our youth theatre, two original musicals and a re-working of an old musical in modern styles. The young people themselves contributed to the music-making. A Youth version of the Musical Theatre Writing Workshop takes place in 2002, funded by the Paul Hamlyn Foundation.

Musical Theatre History at Stratford East

In the 1950s and 1960s Joan Littlewood's Theatre Workshop produced a series of new, populist musicals from a working-class viewpoint. *Fings Ain't What They Used T'be, Make Me An Offer,* and the legendary *Oh, What A Lovely War* began Stratford East's innovations in musicals.

Barbara Windsor and Toni Palmer in *Fings Aint What They Used T'be* (1959)

The drill scene from *Oh, What A Lovely War* (1963)

Josephine Baker depicted in *This Is My Dream* (1987)

Five Guys Named Moe (1990)

Theatre Royal Stratford East Staff

Artistic

Artistic Director	Philip Hedley
Associate Artistic Director	Kerry Michael
Associate Director - Education and Training	Danny Braverman
New Writing Manager	James Peries
Youth Projects Leader	Julia Samuels
Associate Producer	Zoë Simpson
Assistant Producer	Kilian Gideon

Associates (Honorary)

Associate Director	Kate Williams
Associate Writers	Tunde Ikoli
	Patrick Prior
	Paul Sirett
Senior Script Associate	Myra Brenner
Theatre Archivist	Murray Melvin
Assistant Archivist	Mary Ling

Musical Theatre Project

Associate Director	ULTZ
Associate Artists	Paulette Randall
	Clint Dyer
	Fred Carl
	Robert Lee

Aarawak Moon (Visiting Company)

Company Directors	Tracey Daley
	Jo Martin
	Josephine Melville
Drama Project Facilitators	Maxine Brown
	Shakira Henry

Administration

Administrative Director	Belinda Kidd
Administration Manager	Karen Fisher
Theatre Secretary	Sylvie Webb
Development Assistant	Michelle White
Finance Manager	Tina Gardner
Finance Assistant	Barbara Dandy
Finance Assistant	Elizabeth Suchley

Marketing and Press

Head of Marketing and Sales	Caroline Griffin
Community Liaison Officer	Sandra Erskine
Marketing and Sales Assistant	Charlotte Handel
Press Officer (Direct line 020 8279 1123)	Mary Rahman
Press Consultants (Direct line 020 8347 9777)	Sally Homer
(Direct line 020 8340 4443)	Sarah O'Brien

Box Office Manager	Beryl Warner
Box Office Assistants	Asha Bhatti
	Donna Edwards
	Liz King
	Saif Osmani

Front of House

Theatre Manager	Paul R. Griffiths
Bar Supervisor	Brendan McCartney
Catering Supervisor	Elaine Butler
Maintenance/Photography	John Munday
Catering Assistants	Nancy Boateng
	Jacqueline Daly
	Hazel Gibbs
Domestic Assistants	Julie Lee
	Helen Mepham
	Eric Akossou
	Karen Bennett
	Jane Young
Fire Marshalls	Neil Bennett
	Jeremy Haywood
	John Munday
	Andrew Thompson

Ushers Rhoda Akano, Philip Aransibia, Kerri Ash, Kieran Austin, Alison Bigg, Jessica Dickens, Emmanuel Ejay, Sharlene Fulgence, Gloria Gardner, Heather Giles, Rosemary Ikpeme, Lorraine John, Lola Olakunbi, Rameeka Parvez, Sarah Robertson, Abdul Shayek, Jason Thomas, Lynsey Webb, Philbert Xavier

Technical

Production Manager	Felix Davies
Stage Technician	Giles King
Chief Electrician	Stuart Saunders
Deputy Chief Electrician	Ceri Nicholls
Wardrobe Supervisor	Jane Bennett
Stage Manager	Patricia Davenport
Deputy Stage Managers	Nasarene Asghar
	Nina Scholar
	Charlier Parkin
Assistant Stage Manager	Emma Goodway

Board of Directors

Sally Banks, Joanne Campbell, Mary Conneely, Clint Dyer, Shreela Ghosh, Tony Hall (Chair), Illtyd Harrington, Kamaljeet Jandu, Joan Littlewood, John Lock, Murray Melvin (Company Secretary), John Newbigin, Shannen Owen, Mark Pritchard, Kate Williams, Matthew Xia.

First published in 2002 by Oberon Books Ltd.
(incorporating Absolute Classics)
521 Caledonian Road, London N7 9RH
Tel: 020 7607 3637 / Fax: 020 7607 3629

e-mail: oberon.books@btinternet.com

A catalogue record for this book is available from the British Library.

ISBN: 1 84002 280 9

Cover photography: Sharon Wallace

Printed in Great Britain by Antony Rowe Ltd, Reading.

Characters

SANDRA

MANDY

JACKIE

SHENEQUA

BEVERLY

CARRIE

ZOWIE

ACT ONE

Scene 1

Lights up on a dimly-lit shabby-looking locker room. It's in need of a little paint and a good clean. There are five lockers along the back wall. They are all in various states of disrepair: one locker door is tied shut with a shoelace, one has a poster of an alien smoking a joint and another has 'Do Not Enter' scribbled across it. There are four other lockers along side stage left. All the doors on that side are open. In one of the side lockers we see a black bin liner with pink frilly material sticking out. On the floor in front of that locker there is a blue plastic bag. Upstage left between the back and side lockers is the entrance for the toilets and shower room. There is a large 'Out Of Order' sign hanging across the entrance. Also upstage left is a small rickety looking table covered in graffiti. On the table is a ghetto blaster and underneath the table there are two tied up bin bags. There is a long low bench running along the five back lockers. Upstage left there is a small dustbin. Beside the bin is a long wall mirror and above the mirror is a small internal speaker. Along the side stage left is another long low bench, underneath which there is a basket with several net-balls in it. Downstage left is the entrance to the locker room. Downstage right there is a high, small, frosted-glass square window with a chair leaning up beneath it.

Sitting on the back bench there is a plump thirty-something WOMAN looking very dishevelled. Her body is wet and wrapped in a pink bath towel. She is wearing a pair of worn out bedroom slippers. Beside her on the bench she has a large blue sports bag. Her hair is a mess, she is crying and staring into space. Playing low in the background is Frank Sinatra's 'I've Been a Roamer'. The WOMAN gets up and walks over to the ghetto blaster and turns the tape off. She looks around the room solemnly. She walks over to the netball basket and takes one out. She begins bouncing it, dries the tears from her eyes and grips the ball tightly to her chest, standing centre stage. She is interrupted by the TANNOY crackling in and out. We hear a Ragga track, 'If U Man A Gi U Problem.'

TANNOY: Testing! Testing!

We hear a bad feedback and it cuts out. The WOMAN has an alarmed look on her face. She drops the ball and looks at her watch. She walks towards the blue plastic bag on the floor and looks at it for a while. She then takes a deep breath and scornfully picks the bag up. She begins to spin around frantically looking for somewhere to put it. The more she hears the TANNOY, the more nervously she behaves. She looks around at the open locker with the bag of material sticking out, before throwing the bag into the locker and slamming the door shut. The TANNOY kicks in again. This time there is a boy rapping on it.

SECOND TANNOY: Man a man a massive, falla mee, when I chat pon the mikee.

There is a lot of static and the TANNOY cuts out. The WOMAN picks up her bag and exits via the entrance. The TANNOY comes in again.

(*Rapping.*) I knew a girl call Lucy, she was oh so juicy, she had a real tight…

TANNOY: Stop that stupidness boy! You think that is a toy? Go and check the speakers in the…

TANNOY cuts out. We hear the beautiful voice of someone singing very loud off stage left. Another WOMAN, also in her thirties enters wearing a walkman. She is carrying a sports bag and wearing a very brightly coloured head wrap, which has been elegantly wrapped; this is MANDY. She dumps the bag on the floor and takes her jacket off. She goes over to the locker with the alien poster on it and puts her coat in, singing along as she does so. She takes her towel out of the locker, her buff puff and shower gel and walks upstage left to the shower entrance. She looks at the 'Out Of Order' sign and kisses her teeth. She reaches into her pocket and takes out a key. She takes the sign down and rests it on the table, unlocks the door and exits into the room. We hear the shower and the beautiful voice singing 'I'm Every Woman'.

There is the sound of screeching brakes off and the sudden crash of a car. A very harassed looking WOMAN enters wearing sunglasses. She is carrying a sports bag and a plastic shopping bag which she appears to be struggling with.

JACKIE: Fuck! Fuck! Fuck!

She hurries to one of the lockers stage left. She is very out of breath and quickly drops her bags. The TANNOY kicks in again, this time just hissing and crackling. JACKIE looks at the speakers and kisses her teeth. She pulls a vodka bottle from her shopping bag, looks at the label for a few seconds before unscrewing the top and taking a swig. She seems suddenly to become a lot calmer. As she raises the bottle to her mouth to take another swig, we hear a voice. JACKIE quickly puts the bottle back into the plastic bag and then frantically begins to dig in sports bag. She pulls out her gums and quickly stuffs one into her mouth.

We see SHENEQUA, a very fashion conscious looking woman, enter downstage left. She is wearing a tight pair of snakeskin trousers and high heels. She is carrying a 'Louis Vuiton' sports bag. She has one mobile to her ear and another in her other hand. JACKIE is unpacking her bags and putting things into her locker.

SHENEQUA: I'll definitely take care of that for you Mr Hissman, I'll bring all the relevant forms with me on Tuesday, just make sure you have your driver's license and your credit card.

SHENEQUA sounds very sweet and business-like. The phone in her hand begins to ring.

I'm terribly sorry, Mr Hissman, but can I put you on hold for a minute?

She presses button and answers other call.

Yeah, where's my fucking money man! What!? Look, hold on…

27

She switches to other phone.

I wonder if I could call you back Mr Hissman, yes, oh yes, of course, bye for now.

Switches to other phone.

Where's my money?! I want my money, you understand? I want my money, you're fucking with your life, you better...hello! Hello...muppet!

Sound effect of another phone ringing. SHENEQUA drops to her knees and begins digging into her bag. She retrieves the phone and looks at the number. She looks scared, and hesitates before answering. She suddenly focuses on JACKIE. The phone is still ringing.

Alright Jack? Is that your car out there?

JACKIE gets up; she shows SHENEQUA the palm of her hand and exits. SHENEQUA goes upstage to the door, making sure JACKIE's gone, gives the locker room a quick look around, finally answers the phone.

I got rid of everything, I ain't taking no chance, dread, if it all comes on top I'm splurting out, you're breaking up man, hello...hello...

MANDY comes in from the shower room dressed in tracksuit with a shower cap still on her head. SHENEQUA turns around startled, she jumps.

Mandy man! You nearly give me a cardiac.

MANDY: What's up with you?

SHENEQUA: Nutten, is all good.

SHENEQUA goes over to the locker with 'Do Not Enter' written on it and begins packing her things into it.

MANDY: Did you get my tings?

SHENEQUA: Good morning to you too Mandy, yes I did but hear what, it's not like the last ting, it's a little seedy so just give me twenty pounds.

MANDY kisses her teeth and goes to her locker. BEVERLY enters, looking very fit, with a bright coloured tracksuit and matching headband and a towel around her neck. She is sweating and out of breath. She looks at her watch.

BEVERLY: Yes! That's another five minutes off my time, God is good. (*She drops into press-ups.*) God is good one, God is good two.

SHENEQUA and MANDY exchange looks and laugh.

God is good three.

SHENEQUA: The devil is six.

MANDY laughs out loud while changing. JACKIE enters still wearing her sunglasses.

BEVERLY: But God is seven.

She glares at SHENEQUA.

JACKIE: I just tapped Darren's car, he's gonna do his nut, thank God it's just a little dent.

SHENEQUA: (*Laughing.*) Little? You better lose the shades girlfriend.

JACKIE kisses her teeth and walks over to her locker. A very eccentric looking woman enters wearing a tiger print coat and silver ballroom dancing shoes. Her face is very heavily made up and her hair is scooped up into a beehive with an odd looking ponytail at the back. She has a big rucksack on her back and is holding a big orange fluffy diary. She walks centre stage, opens her diary and proceeds to read.

CARRIE: Today's confession: 'I do not have to earn love, I'm lovable because I exist.'

SHENEQUA: That's the same as last week's.

CARRIE: (*Flipping through the pages.*) No, last week's was: 'my heart is open, I allow my love to flow freely.'

MANDY and JACKIE exchange looks. BEVERLY kisses her teeth and SHENEQUA laughs.

I saw Eric today.

BEVERLY: Oh no, Carrie.

MANDY: You're not suppose to go within a hundred yards of his house.

BEVERLY: She must think the judge was joking.

CARRIE: Look some stupid injunction isn't going to keep me from Eric, anyway I didn't go to his house, I was in the park and he jogged past me, it was hard work keeping up with him.

The girls look strangely at CARRIE, but she's oblivious to it all. CARRIE takes her coat off and goes over to the back row locker which is tied with the shoelace. She drops her coat and bag on the bench.

JACKIE: You followed him jogging?

CARRIE: I tried, but these shoes… (*She looks at her silver ballroom shoes.*) …and Eric's ever so fast, but never mind, we'll be side by side before you know it.

MANDY looks up to the skies and mimes 'help'. CARRIE drops into the splits on the floor. BEVERLY goes over to the ghetto blaster.

JACKIE: What about Zowie, has anyone heard from her?

BEVERLY: Yes, she called me yesterday on her way back to London, her mother's out of hospital and she will be here. Can everyone start organising themselves? I'll be warming up in (*She looks at her watch.*) five minutes and I won't be waiting for anyone.

BEVERLY puts on a Soca tape. The music is loud. JACKIE starts to dance, SHENEQUA is making a call on her mobile and BEVERLY is stretching. MANDY goes over to BEVERLY and whispers something.

What!

BEVERLY turns the music off. A thirty-something white woman enters, out of breath and flustered. She's dressed in a very smart tracksuit and is wearing a lot of gold.

ZOWIE: I'm sorry I'm late. (*She sprints past and heads for the toilet.*)

SHENEQUA: Why yu sorry, you're always late.

BEVERLY: (*Turns music down.*) What you saying?

MANDY: I'm saying we need to talk about Sandra, we can't bank on her being here, I know she's Miss Dedication and all that but…well after last week…

ZOWIE enters room.

BEVERLY: She'll be here… Sandra knows we're at a very crucial stage in this tournament, we can win that cup and show everyone that the V.I.P. Crew are back. When can you remember a match that Sandra never turned up to? She buried her father the Friday and turned up to play the Saturday. She'll be here, cos she wants that cup.

SHENEQUA: Well she might get a cup of drinking chocolate that's about it, when last have we trained as a team?

BEVERLY: I don't expect you would know, how often do you turn up? Anyway, we've got this far and I believe we can get further.

CARRIE: Our kits are a disgrace, all the other teams look really classy, Moss Side's are gold and silver, very sophisticated.

ZOWIE: It's not about how we look, it's how we play that matters.

MANDY: Well if you feel like shit, you play like shit.

BEVERLY: I'd just like to say to everyone while Sandra is not here, she is obviously going through a very stressful time right now, we need to all be strong for her.

ZOWIE: She's coming from her honeymoon ain't she?

MANDY: They never had no honeymoon.

ZOWIE: What! Why?

SHENEQUA: They never had no wedding.

ZOWIE is in shock.

MANDY: That bastard Scooty never turned up.

ZOWIE: Raw! That's crosses man, he didn't turn up!?

CARRIE: She was a vision in pink.

SHENEQUA: Shame, the church was ram. (*She laughs and shakes her head.*)

JACKIE: I didn't know she had so many friends.

MANDY: She never knew half those people there, poor thing, remember how she was when he proposed to her.

SHENEQUA: Yeah she didn't get the joke.

CARRIE: She cried for the whole week.

MANDY: And then she got excited and invite the whole community, even that racist milkman.

SHENEQUA: The roller drove her around the block so many times it ran out of petrol and bruck down, woi!

BEVERLY: I was so moved when we were coming out of the church and she stood on the steps and apologised to everyone, as if it was her fault, that's true courage, she could've ran away but she stood her ground, she dug deep and toughed it out.

MANDY: She held it though, I didn't see her cry once.

ZOWIE: Poor Sandra, so weren't any of his mates there?

SHENEQUA: Yeah, Rambo his best man, but he reckoned he never saw him, him lie! He looked guilty!

CARRIE: I tried to cuddle her but she wouldn't let me.

SHENEQUA: Cuddle, she nuh need cuddle, she needed a fucking uzi to blow out the whole day.

MANDY: And then the one Jackie turns up late and start dashing the rice over Sandra.

They all laugh.

JACKIE: Well how was I to know, as far as I was concerned the wedding just finished and she was coming out, and there were people taking pictures.

Everyone looks at JACKIE. They all laugh.

ZOWIE: So what happened?

SHENEQUA: I saw her and her brother walking up the road to the cab office.

JACKIE: I heard the reception was good, imagine people still went.

MANDY: Greedy people man! Free drink and free food…

CARRIE and SHENEQUA look at each other.

CARRIE: It was only going to waste.

The girls turn to look at CARRIE. SHENEQUA looks a bit shady.

I had to go, I was wearing my dancing shoes, even though their weren't much space to dance, it was so ram Shenequa and I couldn't get to buss any moves.

The girls turn to look at SHENEQUA.

SHENEQUA: What!?

BEVERLY shakes her head.

Let he who is without sin cast the first stone.

SHENEQUA looks at BEVERLY. MANDY and JACKIE throw various bits of clothing at and laugh.

ZOWIE: I just hope she's alright.

SHENEQUA: Do you reckon you'd be alright. Yu man leave you at the altar you must feel shame.

MANDY: It ain't about shame, she's hurting, she should've taken things slowly. When she asked me what I thought about it I told her straight, you can't go to Jamaica, and in one week meet a man on the beach who only have one trousers and a pair of trainers with no lace to his name, and honestly take him seriously when he propose to you. Dem man would propose to a donkey if they thought it could get them to foreign. I told her it is just a holiday fling, take it as that and move on.

JACKIE: That's easy to say but look how much years Duffas went without the taste of the man's HOOD! (*Laughs.*) Cor blimey, she must've thought she hit the jackpot when he made a move on her.

ZOWIE: It's just loneliness, I can relate to that with Norman being inside.

MANDY: Her kinda loneliness is way different from yours, she's never had a boyfriend, yes couple of dirty old men who just want to sex her out, but that's it, no man, no kids.

JACKIE: And she ain't no beauty queen.

MANDY: You ain't no Naomi Campbell.

BEVERLY: That's what you find a lot of the times, the ones with the notion that you need to be beautiful have the coldest heart, and are least happy.

SHENEQUA: That one touch you Bev.

JACKIE: Anyway, I think she got off lightly, they could've gone through all that 'get divorced' and then he would've been entitled to half her insurance money and that big dutty house her parents left her.

MANDY: What insurance money! Him nyam that off long time, where you think the designer clothes come from and the bran new car she have him driving up and down in. All she have left is her house, and she's lucky to have that. But I know Sandra, she'd give all that away if she could have her husband and two kids she always talks about.

SHENEQUA: I feel it for her though bwoy, I mean I could half deal with him leaving me for a pork head, but clean out my account! That one woulda kill me dead, for real.

BEVERLY: The lord acts in mysterious ways, he done her a favour, but it's far too early for her to see that.

CARRIE: Well I think she should follow her heart, if she loves him she shouldn't give up, if you focus on what you want, you'll get it.

SHENEQUA: Yeah, like you and Eric, you're focussing on getting him, and he's focussing on getting away from you.

CARRIE: And we're both very happy thank you, and there's still time for Sandra to be.

SHENEQUA: With a yardie! I doubt it, dem Jamaican men are all users, and they think they're so clever, all they want at the end of the day is a passport and some poor sorry old bitch to mind them, yuk! They can grine though.

JACKIE: That's right, that's why I never see you with an African man? Cos you never get it so good.

SHENEQUA: I love my African man, I just like it rough that's all.

ZOWIE: I'm still in shock, I really thought he was nice.

BEVERLY: Well like they say, you can't judge a book by its cover.

SHENEQUA: She would, is black man innit. (*Under her breath.*) Well I ain't lying, I didn't trust him from day dot.

CARRIE: I thought he was gorgeous. Don't you think he looks like the guy in the Halifax ad… (*She sings.*) 'Extra! Extra!' All he needs are the glasses.

MANDY: More like Sooty, he really played the game good though, look how he treated her, breakfast in bed every morning. Freshly squeezed juices, took her all around Jamaica.

JACKIE: And grine two pound of weight off her, but look how she had him locked up from the day he land, I must've seen him twice in that time, both times they were out shopping, Oh, and the time I dropped them to BMW to buy her lovebug, she must've thought we would've wanted him, I don't want no man that comes in a flat box, he has to be ready built, cos there's always a screw or some shit missing.

SHENEQUA: I met a man just like him when I was in Jamaica, I wonder if them related.

ZOWIE: I met a bloke called Denzil in Ochio Rios when I was there in ninety-six, he was so sweet, he called me pinky, and he'd say things to me like, 'come yer pinky, mek mi give yu a stone grind.' (*She speaks in accent.*) He weren't wrong, it was rock hard.

MANDY: You never learn, is Norman me sorry for.

ZOWIE: Sorry for Norman? Please he gives as good as he gets trust me, anyway don't watch me cos yous are no better, we've all done the same thing at some point on holiday, the difference is I call it a fling.

SHENEQUA: Don't compare me to you dear, me nah pay man to fuck me.

BEVERLY: One thing I know is, black man, white man, one legged man or midget man they are all heathens, they are all capable of breaking hearts. Anyway I think we better change the subject, right! The word for the day is focus! We have a very long day ahead of us, it's been a rocky year but by the good grace of God, we've made it to this tournament and we must take advantage of that, our first game is a very crucial one, we're up against the Red Devils.

SHENEQUA: Wha!?

MANDY: Oh yeah, they got relegated didn't they?

JACKIE: Imagine how Trish Roberts must feel, good! She left us to join them and now she has to play her old team to get back up.

SHENEQUA: I'm glad she chipped, she was a rubbish Goal Shooter, Carrie's much better, and look as soon as she joins the Red Devils, dem start lose.

Everyone laughs.

BEVERLY: The Red Devils may be on a losing streak but they're still a formidable team, ladies, they lost their place on the league table and they want it back, they're hungry.

SHENEQUA: Well we're starving.

JACKIE: And I feel greedy.

> *MANDY shakes her head. Offstage we hear the Ziggy Lights chanting, 'The Ziggy Lights come fe wreck, ah how we flex, Ziggy Lights, Ziggy Lights, you ah goh get real bex.'*

BEVERLY: Yes ladies! The Ziggy Lights are in the house, they are in group C, and as we are in group B we need to win at least one of our games in the first round if we hope to play them.

ZOWIE: You know they're gonna be in the finals, they're bound to win all their games.

BEVERLY: Which is why it is so important to get rid of the Red Devils while we're still fresh, thank God we're playing them first, right! The teams in group A are playing first so we've got at least half an hour before our first game, so I suggest we get changed into our kits and...

> *SHENEQUA is inspecting one of the bin liners under the table.*

MANDY: Where are the kits?

SHENEQUA: Oh fuck! (*She opens bag and pulls out a dirty kit.*) Who was suppose to wash the kits last week?

BEVERLY: Oh heavenly father... I forgot to take them home, don't worry, we'll use what we have, don't any of you have an old PE skirt or something?

MANDY: You have one? The last time I played PE was over twenty years ago, the road I lived on don't exist any more much less.

BEVERLY: Well I still have mine.

SHENEQUA: You would!

BEVERLY: Er, what about the rest of you?

SHENEQUA: Look! I'll play in my training shorts.

SHENEQUA is digging through her sports bag.

BEVERLY: (*Clapping her hands.*) Right, I don't want any energy wasted with you worrying about kits, it will sort itself out I know…

The door flies open and all the girls look around at the same time. SANDRA walks in, wearing a powdered pink satin and lace trimmed outfit. She is carrying her overnight bag which she puts into her locker.

SANDRA: Alright girls!

The girls reply in unison. JACKIE begins miming to MANDY.

JACKIE: (*Miming.*) That's the dress.

MANDY: So, you okay, girl?

SANDRA: Yeah, I'm just dealing with it, Mand, trying to forget about it.

MANDY: I'm just happy to see you babe.

SANDRA: So, what's up? (*Looks down at herself and does a twirl.*) So, do you like?

CARRIE: I love the colour.

MANDY: Ye…yes it's…the material's a bit delicate for netball ain't it?

SANDRA: Nah, it's cool, I have one for all of us.

SANDRA goes to the locker stage left and takes out a bin bag. She empties the contents onto the floor to reveal a sea of pink taffeta.

BEVERLY: The Lord is great!

SHENEQUA walks over to the heap on the floor and picks one piece up.

SHENEQUA: This is your wedding dress man!

We hear wedding march and slow fade to blackout…

Scene 2

Lights up on the locker room. SHENEQUA is alone in the room. She has a mobile to her ear and one clipped on to each side of her waist. She's winding up in front of the mirror to the Ragga music ('Dangerous', Barrington Levy) playing in the background. The TANNOY crackles.

TANNOY: Could the Happy Spinsters team captain please report to the judges booth?

SHENEQUA: Mi only have a lickle commercial right now, but I'm picking up some purple H later, yeah, but yu can't get that till after six yu know star, cos…

Her other mobile goes off.

Hole on a minute.

She answers other call.

Hertz reservations, Shenay speaking. How can I help? Oh hi Lisa, yes I've got all the details, two p.m. Gatwick, Mr Clarke, okay thanks for calling Lisa, bye now.

BEVERLY walks in, dressed in her frilly kit. She goes over to the tape and turns the music off. SHENEQUA looks up at her and begins laughing. She continues to laugh hysterically as she walks over and turns the music back on.

BEVERLY: This is not a bashment, you need to leave that ghetto gal attitude at home.

SHENEQUA: (*Still giggling.*) You look fucked up! Black baby Jane. Don't touch my music man!

BEVERLY: I cannot believe it! You're not in your kit and you have time to be frying your brains on that damn phone and wining up in front of the mirror.

SHENEQUA: Warming up! And like I said before, ME-NAH-WEAR-DAT! If you did do your job, we wouldn't have to dress up like eediat in that sad gals wedding dress. (*She begins to walk out.*)

BEVERLY: Shenequa! I'm talking to you.

SHENEQUA: Talk den!

BEVERLY: Why do you have to be so defensive?

SHENEQUA: If you never spent all your time attacking me, I wouldn't have to defend.

BEVERLY: You missed training again on Thursday, where were you?

SHENEQUA: I couldn't make it.

BEVERLY: You have four mobile phones! Use one! If I had known that you couldn't make it I could've simply rescheduled for another day.

SHENEQUA: Don't worry bout me, them lot need the training more than me.

BEVERLY: I am so disappointed, you were one of the few that I thought could leave and go professional, but it's as if you run from opportunity.

SHENEQUA: Oh please Bev, look how much years you played for, and how much times have you been rejected? What have you got to show, apart from couple newspaper cuttings from the Hackney Gazette?

BEVERLY: Listen, I've had some fantastic years playing Netball. I've had my time, it's your time now, netball needs more black players like you.

SHENEQUA: What for?! We ain't going nowhere, how many black players do you know who made it professional? Look at Maxine Mitchell, who could play like her…she had skill and style, and she was more British than Churchill, so if she can't get in, I might as well give up, Chu!

BEVERLY: We just need to be twice as good…

SHENEQUA: Why should I be twice as good, I'm good enough man!

BEVERLY: (*Under her breath.*) To sell drugs.

SHENEQUA: What!? Is people like you send innocent people go a jail, you ever see me sell drugs to anybody? Me have my job.

BEVERLY: I'm not stupid! Your job can't cover your lifestyle, delivering hired cars can't provide Prada shoes and Gucci bags.

SHENEQUA: Yeah, you too red eye, don't watch what I've got, cos I work hard for my things, I'm a hard worker but me nah kiss nobody ass, that's the difference between me and you, I ain't running down what me can't have, that's the road to madness, you know that road.

BEVERLY: As the Lord says, evildoers shall be cut off, but those that wait for the Lord shall inherit the earth, in other words you need to have faith. I came out of the darkness and saw the light.

SHENEQUA: (*Laughing.*) Mmm, there weren't much light in that Mercs the other night.

BEVERLY: What!

SHENEQUA: Well there was enough to see you skinning up your teeth dough, remember Beckton cinema car park? I saw you, with the man's tongue down you throat.

Pause. BEVERLY is in shock.

Just member Bev your God is everywhere, but he'll forgive you, he's used to hypocrites like you, they go to church every Sunday and ask forgiveness for the dutty weekend they've had.

BEVERLY is in shock and lost for words, her face distorts as she seethes with anger.

BEVERLY: Everything that comes out of your mouth is a lie! You wanna persecute me cos you're looking for my attention. Well you've got my attention Shenequa, and that's all you can come with…well thank God I am a Christian, my heart is pure, I fear no evil. (*She licks her finger and dots the sign of the cross as she speaks.*) I'll pray for you dear.

BEVERLY exits. SHENEQUA kisses her teeth, she takes out her phone while looking at the kit. She begins dialling a number, she kisses her teeth again, puts the phone away and picks the kit up from the floor. She holds it up to look at it, shakes her head. She holds it against her body, and looks into the mirror, she laughs.

Blackout.

Scene 3

Lights up on SANDRA alone in the locker room. She is sitting on the chair down stage left, surrounded by the netball kits. She is making some finishing touches to one of the bibs. While stitching she pricks herself with the needle.

SANDRA: Oh shit! (*She looks at her finger before sucking it.*)

TANNOY: Group B will be playing the next match on court two, first up are The V.I.P. Crew versus The Red Devils.

MANDY enters, wearing one of the netball outfits which is a little tight.

SANDRA: Oh wicked! Thank God it fits, I was worried about your chest.

MANDY's breasts are bulging out. SANDRA begins pulling at MANDY's kit, turning her around and giving her a good inspection.

Lift your arms up!

MANDY lifts her arms and we hear the tearing of material.

I was afraid that might happen, don't worry, I have a plan. (*She gets her pins out.*) Do you remember that dress I made for you at Christmas?

MANDY: What there was of it.

SANDRA: You said you wanted sexy.

They both laugh.

MANDY: Have you heard from him?

SANDRA stares at her.

SANDRA: I got my car back.

MANDY: Did he bring it round!?

SANDRA: He wont be driving my car again.

MANDY: I hope you got your keys back, you don't want him turning up using your place like an hotel, better still, change your locks.

SANDRA picks up the Goal Attack bib she's been sewing.

SANDRA: I always wanted to be Goal Attack, best position in the game, no one argues with the Goal Attack, it's like being the singer of a band, all eyes are on you. I just like holding the ball, I never get to hold the ball, I just stand there like a bouncer, just watching and waiting for a moment.

MANDY: You're a good Goal Keeper.

SANDRA: Yeah because I'm big.

MANDY: Your position is just as important as everyone else's, we couldn't play without a Goal Keeper.

44

SANDRA puts on the goal attack bib and does some moves.

SANDRA: You played Goal Attack at school didn't you?
I couldn't get in the team, I tried.

MANDY: You're in a team now girl.

SANDRA: Yeah but look at us, second division, who cares
about second division teams? Do you remember the
Essex Ladies?

MANDY: Do I? Them bitches played like they had wings.

Sound of netball match off.

SANDRA: They played the game with so much grace,
Mand, no team could beat them. I use to watch them
train, they trained like they were in the Army.
Remember Maxine Mitchell?

MANDY: Look, if and when you need me, I will be there
for you, just forget that idiot bwoy, plenty more man deh
a Jamaica, leave him to Jesus.

TANNOY kicks in. Blackout.

TANNOY: Time out!

*Whistle blows off stage. Lights up. Very tight spot on
SANDRA's face.*

SANDRA: The boy at school who sent me a Valentine's
card for a joke, the girls who laughed and called me
Duffas while I sat on my own in the playground, Tina
Hamilton, who used to spit in my food, the women who
don't pay me for the clothes I've sweated over making it
nice for them so they look good, all users and abusers
welcome, leave them to Jesus. (*In Mother's accent.*) The
humblest calf sucks the most milk, rubbish! The
humblest calf dies of starvation, oh God forgive me, I
should've left him to Jesus, he had such sweet words,

only ugly white boys used to look at me, they liked my dark skin and my nappy hair, but I *didn't* like them. There he was carrying my bags to the hotel room, there he was in his crispy white shirt standing in my room, staring at me smiling with his crooked smile, I was truly in Jamaica.

Whistle blows off stage. Lights to black.

TEAM: (*Voices off.*) It's your ball! Wake up Sandra! Oye mark her, Mand!

Blackout.

Scene 4

Lights up on empty locker room. Off stage left we hear jubilant cheers. CARRIE skips in, SHENEQUA and JACKIE follow.

CARRIE: (*Singing.*) I'm pretty, I'm pretty, my Mama says I'm pretty, you ain't got no alibi, you just can't deny, I'm pretty wha wha, I'm pretty.

SHENEQUA: Shut up man! We lost.

CARRIE: I'm sorry! Don't take it out on me darling.

JACKIE: I don't know what the hell Sandra was doing, it was like the girl was sleeping.

SHENEQUA: Well you lot always shout me down when I say she's rubbish.

CARRIE: Come on give her a break, it's only the first game, we done well I think.

JACKIE: I think you need to come off that stupid planet.

SHENEQUA: You must've been in another game, done well!

CARRIE: Well I scored six goals, on my own.

46

SHENEQUA: Yeah and they scored thirty-one, on their own, so that makes us losers, get it!

ZOWIE and MANDY enter the locker room.

ZOWIE: They should've been penalized man, the one that was marking me kept elbowing me, and she deliberately stepped on my toes twice.

SHENEQUA: Oh give it a rest Zowie, you always find something to moan bout…

ZOWIE: I'm not moaning, I'm just saying…

MANDY: It don't make any sense in passing the blame, we played like jerks that's why we lost.

JACKIE: Did you see that hairy face Trisha bitch laughing at our kits?

MANDY: She's just trying to intimidate us, that's how she plays.

ZOWIE: Yeah she kept calling me Horlicks.

BEVERLY enters with a flip chart under her arm, followed by SANDRA savagely tugging at her fingers.

BEVERLY: Can you all gather round please, now! (*She sets up the flip chart.*)

The girls are all staring at SANDRA.

SANDRA: (*Still pulling at her fingers.*) I can't get these frigging rings off my fingers, and they've swollen up from the game.

BEVERLY: Well you know the rules about jewellery, right! Let us not digress please… Sandra, I just want to say, thank you, for being here after all you've gone through and especially for working so hard on our kits. Shame we played like losers. When I said 'leave it to Jesus' I didn't mean let him play the whole game! Now I hope we're all here for the same reasons, to win, we can, all we need to do is play netball, not volleyball. I won't call any names but this is not ballet, Carrie, and I feel one needs to step their pace up a bit, Jackie, and Shen…

SHENEQUA: What you calling my name fa!? How comes you don't mention Mandy, look how much free passes they got cos she stan up wit the ball like she baking bread.

MANDY: Actually it was fu fu, you too full of yuself, you can't take simple criticism, but you always have something to say bout people, just check yourself little girl.

SHENEQUA: At least I ain't afraid to talk the truth, unlike some people.

MANDY: This is just a game, but outside of this, just careful how you deal with me okay.

BEVERLY: If only you lot could use the same amount of energy to play as you do to argue, we wouldn't have a problem. Now can I have some quiet for a minute please!

Everyone looks at BEVERLY.

I had a vision a couple of days ago.

There is a lot of eye rolling and sniggering from the girls.

CARRIE: What did you see Bev?

BEVERLY: I saw a small boy surrounded by a crowd of people. He was holding a bird in his hand attached to a string, he raised his hands up into the air to let the bird fly, but when he let it go, the bird fell flat to the floor, it couldn't fly.

CARRIE: Oh seen.

The girls look oddly at CARRIE and then at BEVERLY.

BEVERLY: I saw us losing, that's what.

SHENEQUA: How positive.

BEVERLY: Yes it was very positive, because based on that vision I now see what needs to be done, I feel it's time to change position ladies.

SHENEQUA goes over to her locker and slams the door.

SHENEQUA: Why change after the first game? We're warmed up now, me nah change that's all me know, I don't care, I'm not changing, before I change I'll go home.

MANDY: Bye!

BEVERLY: Just hear me out first, this is the plan. (*She turns the flip chart.*) Shenequa, you'll play Mandy's position, I think you'll do us more justice in defence.

SHENEQUA: (*Shouting.*) Nah, nah man! I ain't playing no Wing Defence.

BEVERLY: Can I finish please… Mandy you'll play Shenequa's position, Carrie, you go into Centre, I'll play Goal Shooter, Zowie, you and Jackie change, and Sandra you can stay as Goal Keeper.

SHENEQUA: Why do I have to play Wing Defence? That ain't my thing, I'm a attacker not a defender.

BEVERLY: We are all defenders when the opposite team has the ball, and that is something you better understand from now.

MANDY: Well I'm cool playing Goal Attack. It's Shenequa that I can't work with.

SHENEQUA: I can't work with you, you too slow.

MANDY: You have something to prove, God only knows what that is, how you can lob the ball to me, and I'm only a few yards away from you, I don't know.

SHENEQUA: Learn to catch, soh why can't I stay in Goal Attack then?

MANDY: Because I am.

SHENEQUA: Fuck this man!

SANDRA: Oh Jesus Christ!

BEVERLY covers her ears in disgust.

You know what the problem is? We're like seven teams in one, all playing against each other, that's why we can't get nowhere. What difference will it make if we change?

CARRIE: I agree, I don't mind where I play, Centre's good, that way I'm not restricted.

ZOWIE: Yeah, I don't mind changing either Bev.

SHENEQUA: Typical, I don't mind Bev, I'll do it Bev, bend over let me kiss your ass Bev, bloody fa…

BEVERLY: Shenequa!

ZOWIE: What is it with you Shenequa, can't you just allow me to have one opinion?

SHENEQUA: Nah! cos your opinion don't value nutting.

ZOWIE: Every time I open my mouth you're on my bloody case. I wouldn't mind, but I wasn't even talking to you, but it is obvious why you're always on me like this.

SHENEQUA: Really?

ZOWIE: Put it this way, I don't think you'd treat me like this if I was black.

SHENEQUA: Would you let me if I was white?

Crackling sound of TANNOY kicks in. Blackout.

TANNOY: Time out!

Whistle blows off stage. Lights up. Very tight spot on ZO face. The song 'Every Man Do his Thing a Littl Different' plays low in the background.

ZOWIE: I must've been black in another life, I must've been. My sister went to the same school as me, had the same friends as me, but she stayed white… I didn't realise how odd it looked until one day my brother caught me snogging Trench in West Ham Park. He had put up with my cornrow hair, my gold teeth, my head wraps, my gabici's, my dub skirts, he'd even put up with me playing my reggae music with the base thumping… I told him I didn't check anyone's colour and that Trench could've been blue green or red…and you know what he says to me… 'If you're so ~~fucking~~ colour blind, why don't you ever go out with white boys?' I was stumped, I didn't know what to say, I think I just kissed my teeth or something, but he was right. I've never been out with a white brother, all my friends were black, I went to black raves, I had pure black icons on my walls, Malcolm X, Bob Marley, Michael Jackson a map of Jamaica. People say I even try to talk black, talk black, what the ~~fuck~~ Hell is talking black, like all black people talk the same, me just talk how me know. I see other white girls on the black scene and I hate them, they look so odd. I went out the other night and I saw Lucy, this old white woman who's been on the circuit for a while, I remember her from years ago, she looked really good back then. You'd always see her in the front seat of a bimmer with the crissess black man, she looks rough now dough, this old black man had his hand up her skirt, all the black girls were just screwing her and vibing her out, and I thought, is that how they see me? We were the only white people in the shubeene and suddenly I just felt really embarrassed, embarrassed to be white.

Whistle blows off stage. Fade to black.

51

Scene 5

Lights up on locker room. CARRIE and JACKIE are practising moves, throwing the ball back and forth to each other, and doing various passes.

JACKIE: I dunno bout these new positions you know, I really don't see Bev as a Goal Shooter, I thought she would've made me play that position. Oh shit!

Her mobile starts ringing.

Here we go… (*She sighs.*) Hello, hi Da… I know I'm sorry Bev had us held up for ages chatting…yes I know… I said I'm sorry…

MANDY enters. CARRIE throws the ball to her and they begin to play around.

I'm not sure what time we finish, we have a few more matches to play, and we're already running late… actually I was gonna say, the brakes on the car felt really dodgy, I was thinking of dropping it off at the garage when I leave here… No Darren! It's okay, Mandy said she'll give me a lift home…

MANDY looks over and mimes she hasn't got a car.

Darren, I can deal with it I'm not stupid…what! (*Whispering loudly.*) What number? I don't know whose number it is, It could be yours for all you know… Darren… Darren…this is not a good time, I don't know, why don't you phone it then!

CARRIE and MANDY are now on the floor wrestling. MANDY accidentally pulls off CARRIE's pony tail. They crack up laughing. JACKIE begins to wave to them to stop.

(*Giggling.*) Sorry Darren, these girls are messing around …why does it have to be about you! You're getting paranoid, I can't believe it, they were just… Darren? Hello, hello, he hung up… (*Under her breath.*) …fucker.

JACKIE sits quietly and her eyes fill with tears. She quickly dries them and walks briskly over to her locker and takes out her bottle. She drains the remains out before throwing it from a good distance into the bin.

CARRIE: Good goal girl! Is that Darren sending you mad again?

CARRIE stands on a chair and lights her fag, blowing the smoke out the window.

JACKIE: I don't know what his problem is. 'Why didn't you phone? What time do you finish? Who's that in the background?' I can't stand it, it is really pissing me off, then he finds a mobile number and he's stressing me out about who it is! I don't fucking know who it is!

CARRIE: There's something quite sexy about a jealous man ain't there? (*She throws her cigarette out of the window, jumps down off the chair and exits.*)

MANDY: Yeah, when it's a fantasy, Jackie, Jack, cool man, look… You're not dealing with things the right way, you need to fix yourself up, because it looks to me like it is Darren who is keeping you together.

JACKIE: Oh really! Is that what you call, looking through my bags, following me, checking all the calls on my mobile, sniffing my fucking knickers.

MANDY: I hear you, it's all a bit over the top, but you aren't in any position to look after yourself let alone the kids, look at you.

JACKIE: What's that suppose to mean?

MANDY: I saw how you looked when you arrived this morning, the airwaves ain't cutting it no more.

JACKIE: You don't understand.

MANDY: I do, trust me I do, just think! Suppose you had crashed the car on the road with the kids in it?

53

JACKIE: I can't bear being sober around him anymore, and I'll stand up to him after a few drinks.

MANDY: There are other ways of standing up to him, when you're like this you're giving him the upper hand and he knows it.

JACKIE: The thing is, he'd be perfect if he wasn't so bloody jealous and obsessive. I've been with him for half of my life, you would think things would be different by now, it was very flattering when we were younger, but sixteen years two kids and no change.

MANDY: Well why should he change for you when you've already changed for him?

JACKIE: Don't worry, Shayla starts school this year, I'll get my independence back and leave his crusty ass.

MANDY: You're a joker, that's what you said when Shaun was in junior school. If you wanted to leave you would, you obviously love him…

JACKIE: I don't think it's love, it's more like a bad habit, I can't even remember the last time he gave me an orgasm, I just bawl out so that he'll hurry up and get on with it and get off me. Maybe I'm just scared of being by myself, I don't even remember how to pay bills cos he does it all. When you really think about it, I should be happy, serve me right, the two things my Mum warned me about apart from Aids and Babies, short man and small island man, check Darren!

MANDY: Don't you diss my Lucian men, look what your Jamaican man do to Duffas, the best thing for you is to get your Darren some counselling.

JACKIE: (*Laughs.*) Darren! You're mad, he's too clever he'd outsmart them.

MANDY: Monkey know which tree to climb, Darren's too clever for you…this is why I live the way I do, when

I go home I can put the double lock on my door, because nothing ain't getting pushed into my keyhole without me controlling it.

JACKIE: Stop going on like you wouldn't want a relationship again, because everyone does.

MANDY: The purpose of a relationship to me, is company, sex, support and all those wonderful things, I can get all that on demand, when I choose, and that suits me fine, and I'm not frigid, when I need to let off some water, I just pick up the phone, I'm in control, fantastic!

JACKIE: What about love?

MANDY: What love?

JACKIE: You mentioned everything except love.

MANDY: Yeah, I love the sex, I love the support and I love the company, when I choose.

JACKIE: With married men? You're breaking up families for your own convenience, is that fair?

MANDY: Well that's life, married men come after me, and at the end of the day I am after the same thing as them, some good sex. I actually think I keep families together and anyway they're all dogs, take them in feed them and kick their ass out. I'm happy as I am.

JACKIE: Yeah, happy alone.

MANDY: Well at least I can call my life my own, you're just Darren's little puppet.

JACKIE: You having a dig at my Darren? He loves me, a little too much, but he loves me, you know how much women would love my life.

MANDY: Yeah, the ones that have seen the family photo album, but we all say cheese when the photographer says to, don't we.

JACKIE: Don't watch my life Mandy, cos from where I'm standing you ain't got none! What have you got? I've got my family, what you really got?

MANDY: What have I got?! Peace of mind, that's what! You wouldn't know what that is.

JACKIE: Peace of mind! How can you sleep at night! When you had your only child taken from you!

Pause. MANDY looks gutted.

MANDY: Oh, that's where you wanna take it? Go on then, go on, say it, *I was a crack head!* See, I'm not afraid to say it, crack head! Crack head! Crack head! And I lost my daughter because I lost control of my life! I gave it all to Bobby, who you think gave me my first crack pipe?! Bobby!

JACKIE: Well, that's all very sad but Darren looks out for me, that's one thing, he wouldn't do anything to destroy me.

MANDY: Listen to you! You still don't get it do you, you're an alcoholic! A fucking drunk!

JACKIE: Well at least I look after my kids, and that's why God bless me with two. Look at you, do you think God would allow you to bear another child! After how you treated Cora!

MANDY: You fucking evil little bitch!

MANDY stands up and walks directly over to JACKIE who is staring at her wide-eyed. She goes straight up to her and swings a punch hitting JACKIE in the mouth. They both react shocked. JACKIE rubs her lips and looks at her hand for blood.

JACKIE: Oh my god! You hit me, you fucking hit me!

JACKIE rushes towards MANDY and slaps her back hard. MANDY grabs JACKIE by her throat and JACKIE holds

MANDY's hair. The girls are striking at each other wildly and most of the time they are missing blows. JACKIE has MANDY on the floor and is on top of her trying to push her finger in her mouth. MANDY bites JACKIE and is now on top. They are beginning to look tired and sloppy. They are now by the lockers stage left. MANDY pulls herself up from the floor resting one hand hard on JACKIE's head to help her up. JACKIE quickly springs up from the floor. MANDY swings a right punch and at the same time JACKIE opens one of the lockers to block it. MANDY's fist connects with the locker knocking it back into JACKIE's face. They both shout out together in pain. The girls break down laughing as they tend to their wounds. They are both out of breath and breathing heavily.

JACKIE: You…stupid…bitch, have I…g…ot a bump on my he…ad.

JACKIE pauses as she catches her breath. She shows MANDY her head.

MANDY: (*Wiping away the tears of laughter.*) Your head's alright, look at my knuckles.

JACKIE: I roughed you up though, talk the truth.

MANDY: You'd love to think so wouldn't you? The only lick I got was from the stupid locker door. You still as clumsy as ever.

JACKIE: What!? You forget the first thump I give you?

MANDY: That was nothing, that felt like when I powder my face, you forgot your first thump? Bamb! (*She does the action with her fist in her hand.*)

They both laugh. JACKIE goes to her locker and takes her bottle out. She takes a sip and hands it to MANDY who declines.

JACKIE: How old is Cora now Mand?

MANDY: Big woman now, she's sixteen next month. I'm just glad we're still talking man, she knows I love her, she doesn't come around much but the counsellor says to give her time.

JACKIE: Once she can make that move on her own, she'll be all over you, don't worry.

ZOWIE rushes in.

ZOWIE: Jack! Mand! Come quick, fight! fight!

Both girls rush out.

Blackout.

Scene 6

Lights up on locker room. SANDRA is sitting looking dishevelled. Her hair is a mess and her bib is torn and hanging off one shoulder. She is heaving and puffing heavily. All the girls are surrounding her. A voice shouts from outside 'C'mon you fat slag! Come out then! Butch bitch!' SANDRA attempts to get up but the girls hold her down, practically sitting on top of her.

JACKIE: (*Rubbing SANDRA's back.*) You alright Sang? What happened man?

CARRIE: I don't know what happened, I went into the store room and I saw Sandra holding Trisha in a headlock.

SHENEQUA: That was so wicked! She took some rawted licks, good!

ZOWIE: They're threatening to call the police aren't they?

SANDRA: Good! She can call the fucking army for all I care, I'm ready for them! Bitch! She's lucky she's still breathing, I wanted to thump out her heart, I've had enough of all the bitches around here and they know who they are.

The girls look at each other.

MANDY: Who saw? Was anyone there?

ZOWIE: Nah, just me and Carrie and then one of her mates helped us to break it up, that's when I came for you two.

MANDY: Well that's cool, we'll just deny it, by the way Sandra, I think you should go home, you're not ready to be dealing with all this.

SANDRA: Dealing with all what… I'm alright, so you can all stop crowding around me like I'm a fucking freakshow. Why is it you always think you know what is right for everyone! Bout go home. (*She kisses her teeth.*)

Sirens can be heard passing the building. SHENEQUA suddenly panics and sprints to her locker. She takes a bag out and rushes to the bathroom. SANDRA becomes very edgy, drops her head and notices a spot of blood on her arm.

(*Screaming.*) Please get it off me! Get it off. (*She becomes hysterical.*)

MANDY: Shit! Carrie, get me the first aid box please…it's okay, Sandra…look it ain't even your blood…see.

CARRIE walks over sternly. She hands MANDY the first aid box, straddles SANDRA and slaps her hard two times across her face. SANDRA is in shock and stares CARRIE in her eyes. The girls attempt to pull CARRIE away but she shrugs them off. SANDRA then grabs her viciously around her neck. CARRIE looks her in her eyes, gently pulls SANDRA towards her and cuddles her. Strangely she calms down. SHENEQUA rushes back sweaty and dodgy looking.

SHENEQUA: Is the beast dem gone yet?

JACKIE: What beast, there's no beast out there you goof.

SHENEQUA: Oh almshouse man! I thought I heard the…

JACKIE: I thought you looked a little light skinned, are you wanted?

JACKIE walks over to the back bench and sits.

MANDY: (*Laughing.*) Check it though, big time dealer and look what the sound of a siren do to her.

SHENEQUA takes her mobile out and begins to make a call.

ZOWIE: (*Looking outside.*) Raw, Bev's talking very hard to the stonefaced umpire.

JACKIE: Well we're finished now, cos she's a racist bitch.

ZOWIE: She's black.

JACKIE: So?

SHENEQUA: She's like you Zowie, she don't like her own.

MANDY: Chill out noh, can you see Trisha?

ZOWIE: Yeah, she's talking to the umpire as well.

JACKIE: (*Walks over and stands behind ZOWIE.*) Look at her limping like something's wrong with her leg.

CARRIE: Does she look bad.

JACKIE: She's trying to look bad, she's alright.

ZOWIE: Ere, that's your Darren innit Jack? He must be looking for you, ere! (*She shouts.*) Darren!

JACKIE: Don't call him over here you fool.

ZOWIE: Sorry, it's not like he don't know you're here.

JACKIE: So what!? Shenequa quick do us a favour, go out there and tell Darren that I've gone out…no!…tell him I'm with Bev…no, just tell him I've popped to the shops!

SHENEQUA: Just tell the bwoy fe fuck off!

JACKIE looks at SHENEQUA.

Joke! I'll go.

SHENEQUA walks towards the exit. As she is about to open the door, it flies open and in walks BEVERLY. SHENEQUA slips past her and heads out.

BEVERLY: Where you going?

SHENEQUA: (*She shouts back.*) Two minutes man.

JACKIE: See what I mean, the bastard's suppose to be at work, what does he want now. He really pisses me off at times, that's the second time he's turned up stalking me.

BEVERLY: Well, I don't know what happened out there but luckily for Sandra, neither does anyone else. It's her word against yours, she's got a few scratches but she'll be alright.

SANDRA: I don't give a shit! She love running up her mouth too much, she's lucky she have a leg to walk on. I've had enough of her, and I've had enough of people pissing over me and treating me like a piece of shit. Those days are done, you hear me, bout she's laughing at my kit.

BEVERLY: Your kit? This was over a kit? Listen. It is far better to kill with kindness. What you need to understand Sandra is, we are not just a team, we are a family, and it is fine if you don't wish to talk to us about anything, but I want to let you know, that we are all here for you, whenever you need us, and I speak for all of us, I think it is mighty courageous for you to go through what you did and still be here today.

SANDRA: Where else have I got to go?

BEVERLY squeezes her hand.

SHENEQUA enters with the mobile still stuck to her ear.

JACKIE: What did he say? Is he gone? He ain't seen the car has he?

SHENEQUA: Him smell sweet bwoy, I can taste the aftershave in mi mout, anyway yu lucky! He walked straight past the car and he didn't notice a thing. He said to tell you that he's working late and that he's left the kids with his sister...oh and to wish you luck.

JACKIE: That's why he came here? I spoke to him three hundred times already today, him couldn't just tell me that then?

SANDRA gets up quickly. The girls hesitate to grab her, unaware of what she is about to do. She looks at them and raises one hand in the air, indicating 'leave me alone'. She takes a bin bag from under the table and begins digging into it.

SANDRA: You can have these back. Here you go Jackie ...that's yours.

JACKIE: No man, I don't want it back.

SANDRA: Mandy, here.

MANDY: Sandra, cool it man, just keep them they're yours.

SANDRA: Shenequa, here you go...that's yours...Bev.

SHENEQUA: Ta. (*She puts the gift into her locker.*)

BEVERLY: Sandra, please,those gifts are for you irrigardless, we all chose those gifts with you in mind.

SANDRA: Yeah, well I don't want them, you might as well take them back because they'll only end up in the bin with all the other sore reminders... Carrie, there you go.

BEVERLY: Okay, how about giving it to a charity, my Church is trying to raise money to build an extension, I'll take them, I can sell them.

SANDRA: Do they want a house and a car as well?

MANDY: Come on, stop talking stupidness man.

SANDRA: Stupid! Yeah that's what you all think isn't it,
stupid Duffas! Who's gonna stay with her, none of you
liked him, you all sat around chatting us, bout how he's
using me...well you all fucking use me! So what's the
big deal, plait this head, sew this dress, put in weave,
baby-sit, bake cake. I'm everyone's fucking skivvy, and
that's what pissed you all off, Sandra started to say 'no'.
Well you all got what you wanted. I'm a single lonely
sad bitch again like you lot.

Everyone is shocked to silence.

You lot couldn't even give him a chance, he was right,
you're all a pack of jealous bitches! Just cos I found a
life, you all think you're so fucking perfect don't you,
well I've got you sussed.

The girls' expressions change from shock to humour.

(*Referring to SHENEQUA.*) Yeah, roll your eyes! You're
just an afrocentric Nigerian yardie wannabe, who have
more mouth than moisturiser.

MANDY smirks.

And you're no better, you think you're mother fucking
Theresa and all you do is fuck people's man for a bag a
weed, and you! (*Referring to JACKIE.*)

JACKIE: Don't even go there cos I never tied down your
man and stop him from marrying you.

BEVERLY: Please Jackie...keep it calm.

JACKIE: Nah man! We've been at her side from day one
and now she's flipping out on us because he turned out
to be a slimy bastard.

63

It becomes silent as SANDRA begins to break down.

SANDRA: (*She cries.*) He told me he loved me…and I really believed him. He took me to meet his parents, they were so nice. Why would he do that, why would he take me to meet them if he didn't love me, why?

BEVERLY: Come now, he may love you still, but love is a strange thing, there could be a million and one reasons why he didn't turn up.

SHENEQUA: True, he could be dead for all you know.

The girls all look at SHENEQUA. SANDRA stops crying suddenly.

BEVERLY: Listen once everything has cooled down, you should arrange to meet him and just ask him why.

JACKIE: Why? Cos Sandra ain't got no money left, him nyam her out dry and just true him hear say that white gal won the lottery, him gawn, he's a dutty whoring bastard, he left her for a stinking white gal, no offence Zowie.

ZOWIE: None taken, I don't stink.

MANDY: Why don't you go away for a while Sandra, just to get away from everything and get out of that house? You're quite welcome to stay with me if you like.

SHENEQUA: On no, you'll come out of there with your head turned the other way around with her ju ju crap.

MANDY: If I was into ju ju, I would've made you a mute long time.

SANDRA: I'll be okay, you don't want a bag of crosses following you, that's all I seem to carry, crosses.

BEVERLY: Listen, there is a good reason behind everything that happens, life is a journey, and we are the vehicle.

Anything can happen en route, you could run out of petrol, you could turn down the wrong road, you could…

SHENEQUA: Have a write-off.

BEVERLY: (*She stares at SHENEQUA.*) The point is, you live, you learn and it gets better. Look at what I had to go through, especially after John left, I felt like you're feeling now, all the worst feelings, but I found Christ and now I have many children, many brothers, sisters, mothers…

SHENEQUA: (*Laughing.*) Ministers.

BEVERLY: So! (*Exaggerated loudness.*) All I'm saying is don't let one bad moment ruin all the others.

SHENEQUA: You should take her church with you Bev, find her a good honest faithful Christian man, innit.

TANNOY kicks in.

TANNOY: Could Beverly Scott go to the main hall please?

BEVERLY: (*Walks towards exit.*) I will take heed to my ways, that I sin not with my tongue: 'I will keep my mouth with a bridle, while the wicked is before me.' Psalm 39. (*She exits.*)

Scene 7

Lights up on locker room. MANDY, JACKIE and ZOWIE are in the locker room. JACKIE is sitting on the chair in front of MANDY who is plaiting her hair. ZOWIE is looking in the mirror with a hand resting on her stomach.

MANDY: You're pregnant?

ZOWIE: Tell the whole street why don't you!

JACKIE: How did you manage that? Norman's inside.

ZOWIE: I know it's a long story, actually, no it's rather short.

Sounds of game off. Loud cheering, whistle blowing.

JACKIE: You dirty little bitch.

ZOWIE: I blame the Tequilas and Champagne. I vowed I would never drink again after that night. Remember the time I went to the Morgan Heritage concert and met up with my ex, Marvin.

JACKIE: What you fucked him and never used a condom!?

ZOWIE: I wouldn't mind but I was so pissed I don't even remember the sex, I just woke up naked and sore.

JACKIE: So how much pregnant are you?

ZOWIE: Well if my calculations are right, I could be about eight weeks.

JACKIE: What about Norman, what you gonna tell him, and does this Marvin bloke know that he's gonna be a dad?

ZOWIE: Nah! you're mad, nah mate, I've got a little plan that I'm working on.

MANDY: You really take life for a joke, suppose it was Aids that you caught.

ZOWIE: Don't say that! (*She makes the sign of the cross.*)

MANDY pats JACKIE on her back, indicating she's finished her hair. JACKIE gets up off the chair and walks over to the mirror inspecting her hair. MANDY builds a spliff.

JACKIE: So what's this plan then, you gonna have an abortion?

ZOWIE: Oh no way! I'm a Catholic, I'm gonna work on Norman.

MANDY: When is he coming out anyway?

ZOWIE: He should've come out ages ago, but he got into another fight and broke this bloke's nose and got twelve weeks added to his sentence. That's the third fight he's had in there. But like I said, I've got a plan so I need to keep him sweet cos he's due to come out for a day next week, and I don't want him messing up.

JACKIE: Well, spit it out then.

ZOWIE: Well… I know you two will think I'm mad but… When he comes out next week, I'm gonna give him a bit, and then a couple of weeks later, I'll tell him that I'm pregnant.

MANDY: You mad…every idiot knows pregnancies last for nine months.

JACKIE: (*Laughing.*) He'll just work the dates out won't he?

ZOWIE: We're talking about Norman here.

JACKIE: You're right, he ain't the brain of Britain is he? Well I'll give up the booze if he falls for that one.

ZOWIE: Well, ear what! between me and you two right… (*Pause.*) Brandy ain't Norman's.

JACKIE: Rawted! You lie.

ZOWIE: Serious, her dad lives in Croydon.

JACKIE: Poor Norman.

ZOWIE: Don't say it like he's suffering, at the end of the day we love each other and that's all that matters.

MANDY: You're not easy boy, but Norman thinks she's his don't he?

ZOWIE: He loves her to bits, even if he knew it wouldn't matter now.

MANDY: So what about Gin? Is he Norman's?

67

ZOWIE: Course he is, you just have to look at him, he's the image of his dad.

MANDY: Bwoy, so you gonna give the poor man another jacket?

ZOWIE: Yeah well I'm giving him what he wants, he wants more children so he'll be happy for it, it's not my fault he's been firing blanks is it. I just have to pray he doesn't get himself into any trouble by next Saturday otherwise all my plans will crash.

MANDY: You better say a big strong prayer girl, cos you're playing serious games.

ZOWIE: Speaking of games, what are we gonna do about the drinks?

CARRIE walks in briskly. She goes directly to her locker and takes out her recorder. She flexes her fingers and exercises her mouth, licks her lips and slowly puts the recorder to her mouth and begins playing 'Three Blind Mice'. She plays the same notes over and over again.

JACKIE: Carrie please! You're doing my brain in man.

SHENEQUA puts her head around the door.

SHENEQUA: Bev said to tell you lot we've got fifteen minutes.

The girls get busy grabbing for the floor mats and stretching. JACKIE gets down into a stretch which leads into the splits.

JACKIE: Fucking hell! My leg! (*Screws her face up in pain.*)

JACKIE limps over to the bench. CARRIE rushes to tend to her. She begins massaging JACKIE's calves.

ZOWIE: Here we go, toilet again. (*She goes to shower room.*)

CARRIE: I'd check my bladder out if I was you Zowie, you've been in and out of that toilet all morning.

68

SHENEQUA: Maybe she's got a dose. (*She laughs.*)

JACKIE: You see how them white girls are different though.

MANDY: Yeah, different in colour.

JACKIE cuts her eyes at MANDY.

JACKIE: Wait until she brings him a Chinese baby, serve him right for being so thick.

A mobile is ringing loudly from one of the lockers.

Shenequa pass my phone for me, one guess who that is.

SHENEQUA hands her the phone.

Hello…hello.

SHENEQUA: So what's up with Zowie then?

MANDY: You're too nosey.

JACKIE's expression begins to change drastically. She has the phone pressed to her ear but she isn't speaking. She tries to shake CARRIE off her legs and stands up briskly. CARRIE is behind her, still rubbing her legs.

SHENEQUA: You might as well tell me cos I think I know what it is anyway.

MANDY: Here we go.

SHENEQUA: So you're not gonna give me lickle scandal.

MANDY: You too fast, anyway you got two more of those twenty bags? I have a visitor coming over tonight.

SHENEQUA: Well, er… (*Stuttering.*) I…not quite.

MANDY: You couldn't done all that gear already.

ZOWIE comes from the bathroom holding up a plastic bag dripping with water.

ZOWIE: Is this yours? It was floating in the toilet.

SHENEQUA looks shocked. The girls crack up laughing.
They begin to inspect the bag. JACKIE is leaning awkwardly
against the wall. She kicks at CARRIE who is still on her
legs. The door flies open and in walks BEVERLY. SANDRA
follows with a basin full of cut oranges. She stops suddenly
,sniffing the air. ZOWIE quickly throws the wet bag in
MANDY's lap, who throws it to SHENEQUA, who quickly
throws it to JACKIE. JACKIE's face is in a state of shock,
she doesn't respond and CARRIE does a flying jump and
catches the bag. She throws a good shot into the bin. BEVERLY
watches them not knowing what is being thrown around.

Is everything okay, Ja...

JACKIE: Shoosh man! (*Waving her arms and pressing the*
phone even harder to her ear.) That's it! That's it now!

She ends her call and begins pacing up and down slowly,
holding her head, confused, standing, kneeling, sitting. She
then gently places the phone into her bag, walks over to her
locker, takes out her bottle wrapped in brown paper, unscrews
the cap and gobbles it down. She picks up a foot of shoe, puts
it down. She then opens CARRIE's locker and takes out a
baseball bat and calmly walks out unnoticed.

BEVERLY: (*Still sniffing.*) Who's been smoking!? Carrie,
Zowie, Mandy!

MANDY: I'm innocent.

CARRIE is on the floor in a backbend position. She raises up
into a crawl and crawls over to BEVERLY in that position
and stands up directly in front of her.

CARRIE: It was me, and I...

A crashing sound is heard offstage and a car alarm is going
off. Everyone's face is still.

As I was saying, it's been a very stressful time in here, and…

One loud crash and the alarm stops.

BEVERLY: (*Hands on her ears.*) Carrie you know this is a no smoking building. I am sick and tired of telling you lot not to smoke in here, therefore, as from now, five pounds fine for anyone found smoking.

The girls moan.

Right now! Focus! We are going to have to play like lions. We know that team is very quick, extremely skilful.

ZOWIE: And bloody rough.

SHENEQUA: I ain't fraid of them, I'll bust their ass from any position mate.

BEVERLY: Is it possible for you to shut your mouth up for just one minute?

SHENEQUA: Just one more thing before I do, I forgot to tell you…

BEVERLY: Let's deal with the game shall we Shenequa? Everyone knows their positions, nothing changes, let us work together in this one. Man to man tactics for this one girls, are we ready?

The girls shout out with energy.

Let us pray.

The girls gather round reluctantly. Lots of kissing of teeth and grumbling.

Dear Lord, we thank you for giving us the opportunity to be here today. Dear Lord, bless the floor upon which we're about to walk, bless the ball we're about to bounce, bless the net we're about to score in. Dear Lord we give ourselves to you, and hope that you will take us through. Yes Lord, we pray for Trisha Roberts, and all alike, Lord we pray for the opposing team, we pray they can accept defeat. Thank you Lord. Amen.

The girls all repeat Amen.

Okay let's go! Shoot to win!!

The girls scream in a circle and go into a fast jog on the spot. They all stop together. MANDY puts one arm into the air and begins singing.

MANDY: Lift up your head and hold it up high, we know that we'll win the fight.

The others all put their hands up and join in.

BEVERLY: V.I.P. C.R.E.W (*Repeat.*) V.I.P. Crew are here to play. (*Repeat.*) You ain't getting no free pass. (*Repeat.*) We're just here to kick your ass. (*Repeat.*)

They all chant as they jog out to play. SANDRA jogs out of the line, she kneels and signs the cross on her chest. As she stands JACKIE rushes in looking very red-faced and messy. She walks straight past SANDRA, opens her locker and takes a small swig. She pushes her hair back with her hands.

SANDRA: What are you doing?

Silence.

What's going on man?

JACKIE: That stinking little shortass man Darren is only having an affair, can you believe it, after all he puts me through, always accusing me of fucking around.

SANDRA: (*Looking concerned.*) Never! Shit, I'm sorry man.

JACKIE: You're sorry! Darren's gonna be sorry, I'm going to my mum and dad's tonight with the kids. Darren can go to hell. I just can't believe it. What have I ever done to him…bwoy Sandra I'm sorry man, you don't want to hear this.

SANDRA: Nah it's cool man, just don't blame yourself. How you feeling?

JACKIE: Just like you.

Silence.

I feel I could kill a bloodclaut man today.

Whistle blows off stage. Fade to black.

The locker room changes into a netball court. The girls are in their positions doing various choreographed moves. The other team has the imaginary ball. The V.I.P. Crew are defending their net. We hear people cheering from the sidelines, then focus on the imaginary ball as it goes into the net. We hear the sound of the ball hitting the net. The girls get the ball. It should look like a well choreographed dance as they work the ball to the other net to score.

SHENEQUA: Who wants it!?

ZOWIE: Shenequa!

MANDY: Pass the ball!

BEVERLY: Carrie! Wake up!

JACKIE: To me, to me!

CARRIE: Bounce it!

SHENEQUA: Don't drop it man!

SANDRA: It's my ball!

We see MANDY trying to score and failing. The other team gets the rebound. V.I.P. Crew run to defend their net using all their defence to mark the other team. V.I.P. Crew move down the court quickly and skilfully. They pass the ball around looking for a gap to strike. CARRIE dodges an opponent and gets the ball. She tries to pass the ball, but no one is free, so she decides to go for a shoot. Everything goes into slow motion. SHENEQUA covers her eyes, BEVERLY looks like she's praying, MANDY is punching the air and JACKIE is puffing heavily. ZOWIE is trying to dodge her opponent and jumps high for CARRIE to pass the ball, while SANDRA has both fingers crossed.

ZOWIE: Carrie! Ere! Carrie! Oh, shit! That's a foul man!

SHENEQUA: Foul man! Foul! You know that!

Blackout.

End of Act One.

ACT TWO

Scene 1

Lights up on locker room. The whole team are gathered except JACKIE. They all look exhausted. ZOWIE has a flannel on her head and BEVERLY is lying flat out on the back bench. MANDY has a packet of frozen peas on her knee, SANDRA is comforting CARRIE who is crying and SHENEQUA is pacing the floor. The room is quiet apart from the odd kissing of teeth. The TANNOY crackles.

TANNOY: Could all the losers from group A and group B please report to the judges booth to pick up their medals?

CARRIE: Oh we still get a medal?

JACKIE: Yeah, the loser's medal.

SHENEQUA: Carrie! Come here, pretend you're me, right. Mandy had the ball looking for me, I manage to dodge the knock-knee gal marking me, I call out to Mand, we make eye contact and she passes the ball, the next thing I know, that knock-knee bitch karate chop me in my neck. That's a deliberate foul, that umpire must be fucking blind man.

MANDY: We would've won that game if the foul had been called.

SHENEQUA: I was shocked when I didn't hear the whistle.

ZOWIE: We gave that game away man, we just let them score that last goal.

MANDY: Yeah, because we're thinking foul, game going to stop, free goal shot to us.

BEVERLY: That doesn't mean we stop playing! I was the only one still marking my man. If the umpire didn't see it, it never happened, that's the rules.

SHENEQUA: But you saw it, Bev, you didn't even go and reason with her, you're the bloody coach ain't you?

BEVERLY: And say what? (*In a childlike tone.*) 'Oh that's not fair.'

Sound of JACKIE throwing up in the toilet.

SHENEQUA: That's another thing, why did you let her play? We would've been better off playing with six than have that drunkard messing up the game, that's why the umpire didn't see the foul cos she was too busy watching Jackie's antics.

ZOWIE: Boy, she was freaking me out, she kept marking me, and I had to keep saying 'Jack, it's me, Zowie.'

SANDRA: She's got a lot on her mind.

SHENEQUA: Yeah well it's very sad about her man and that, but we've all got problems, you don't bring your problems to the game, you get me?

JACKIE staggers out of the shower with a wet face.

MANDY: You finish decorate the toilet?

JACKIE: Anyone got a mint?

MANDY: You need some cerasee tea in your blood.

SHENEQUA: She need AA, believe.

JACKIE: Don't fuck, you hear me don't fuck!

SHENEQUA: Come outa my face with you stinking mout.

Loud chanting of the winning team can be heard off.

BEVERLY: I think we need to call a meeting for early next week. I know you're all feeling rather disappointed right now, but as I always say, the Lord works in mysterious ways, we just have to pray.

CARRIE: I know! Why don't you pray for a miracle, Bev?

They all look at CARRIE with pity.

No, I'm serious.

MANDY: We know.

Offstage a whistle is blown. We hear cheering (chanting Ziggy Lights) going past the locker room.

ZOWIE: Sounds like the Ziggy Lights won the game.

SHENEQUA: We should be playing them, man.

BEVERLY: Don't worry, next time we will.

SHENEQUA: Netball ain't about next time for me, this time is what matters, the present not the future.

SANDRA: I won't be around next time anyway.

JACKIE: What! She's leaving.

BEVERLY: You can't leave us, things aren't so good now but it can only get better.

SANDRA: I'm going away.

CARRIE: You're leaving!? Oh my god! Can I have her locker when she leaves.

TANNOY crackles.

TANNOY: Will the V.I.P. Crew's Team coach report to court three immediately. Thank you.

BEVERLY: Look, I need to talk to you all before you leave, can everyone just wait, please? (*She leaves the room.*)

Everyone is milling around, getting dressed and slowly packing their bags. MANDY goes into the shower and begins singing 'Rainbow Country'.

SHENEQUA: I ain't hanging around, she's lucky, she ain't got a home to go to.

JACKIE: We may as well wait to see what she has to say.

CARRIE: I think she's gonna quit netball.

SANDRA: She's never gonna give up netball.

JACKIE: Shenequa, hold on a minute, which way you going? You can give me a lift.

SHENEQUA: Nah man, I have to hit the streets, I'll drop you to the bus stop.

JACKIE: It's outside the building.

ZOWIE: I'll give you a lift.

SHENEQUA: There you go, and she'll wait for you till next week and bring you back too won't you dear?

BEVERLY comes rushing back. MANDY comes out of the toilet.

BEVERLY: God is great! Get your kits back on, we're in girls!

MANDY: Wha...why...

BEVERLY: Not now, I'll explain later just get ready and warm yourselves up.

ZOWIE: But Bev!...

BEVERLY takes her whistle from her locker and blows hard.

BEVERLY: Not now! get ready, the V.I.P. Crew are back!

JACKIE's mobile starts ringing.

JACKIE: It's Darren. (*She answers the call.*) Darren...fuck off! Right, fuck off! I'm playing netball.

Scene 2

Lights up on locker room. CARRIE and MANDY are crowded around watching the playback on a small video camera. The crackling sound of the TANNOY kicks in.

TANNOY: The Happy Spinsters have just been disqualified due to foul play, The V.I.P. Crew have been reinstated, BOOM!

MANDY: That's a living karate chop man!

CARRIE: Rewind it.

SHENEQUA: Look at the shock on my face.

MANDY: It's all there in beautiful colour, the umpire couldn't argue with that.

SHENEQUA: Your sister pulled a master stroke there!

CARRIE: Terrible camera work, I mean, she needs light, you can barely make out anyone's features it's so dark, and it's very shaky.

MANDY: Don't be dissing my sister, she only just got the camera, she's learning, and anyway she done us a favour.

CARRIE: Oh, I see, this is her debut.

MANDY: What!

CARRIE: Her first film.

SHENEQUA: Look! If it wasn't for Chloe we wouldn't be playing the Ziggy Lights right about now, we'd be sitting at home watching Brookside.

CARRIE: No we wouldn't, it doesn't start till ten past five.

ZOWIE and JACKIE enter. SANDRA comes out of toilet.

SANDRA: Them toilets stink man, ain't we got any bleach, don't these toilets get clean anymore?

JACKIE: Not when there's an out of order sign hanging across it.

SHENEQUA: This is the biggest changing room and the only reason we have it and not the visiting team is because they think the shower's out of order, so…

SANDRA: I know the coo, so that means you can't clean the toilet?

SHENEQUA: Can't you?

SANDRA: I've been cleaning these toilets for years and no one else ever offered to do it, but look, as soon as I stop it's stink and dirty.

ZOWIE: You never had to do that Sandra.

SANDRA: Oh, didn't I?

CARRIE: I'll clean the toilet.

JACKIE: No! I'll clean it.

ZOWIE: I'll clean the toilet.

SHENEQUA: Nah, let me, I insist.

They are mock fighting trying to get to the toilets as BEVERLY walks in.

BEVERLY: Ladies, ladies please, we have at least (*Looking at her watch.*) fifteen minutes before we face the enemy. I just ventured past the enemies' changing rooms, and they are discussing tactics, preparing moves, planning attacks, they are like soldiers, but we have to be the terrorist. (*She goes over to tape machine.*)

SHENEQUA: I'm a hit man.

JACKIE: I'm the terminator.

CARRIE: I'm spiderman.

SHENEQUA: You play like a spider.

Loud Soca music blares out. JACKIE holds her head. ('Who Let the Dogs Out?', original version.) BEVERLY is doing some serious Soca moves. Everyone attempts to follow her. They start off looking very messy then it turns into a great warm up routine incorporating netball moves. We hear cracking of thunder and lightning.

TANNOY kicks in. The sound is crackling in and out with a lot of static. BEVERLY turns the music down and tries to listen. The girls are out of breath.

TANNOY: Play…suspended…. (*The voice is coming in and out until it cuts out.*) …til further notice.

SHENEQUA: What the fuck was all that about?

TANNOY: (*Static.*) Rain has suspended play, so… (*It cuts out again.*)

BEVERLY: This is a minor set back, ladies, we are still in it, and you must be in it to win it! I will lift up mine eyes onto the hill from whence cometh my help, Psalms 121.

SHENEQUA: This is long man.

JACKIE: I've got to pick up the kids.

BEVERLY: Look, it's still only… (*She looks at her watch.*) …three-thirty, that cloud is definitely on the move, I doubt it will rain for long, it has been threatening all morning so just as well it's happened now. I'd rather that than it being in the middle of our game.

CARRIE: But we've played in the rain before, Bev.

MANDY: And I bloody hate it, mess up my hair man.

ZOWIE: That's not rain, Carrie, that's a storm out there.

BEVERLY: (*Looking at SHENEQUA.*) Where are you off to?

SHENEQUA: Shoot some pool man.

MANDY: I'll play you.

SHENEQUA: Cool, yu want to lose yu money, two pound a game yu know.

JACKIE: (*Jumps up brightly.*) The bar's open!?

JACKIE goes over to her locker and begins changing into her track bottoms.

BEVERLY: Do you think it's wise to go to the bar, Jackie? Why don't you have a coffee?

JACKIE: What is this? What are you my fucking mother? Don't start with me.

BEVERLY: Please Jackie, look, I don't happen to think anyone should be going to the bar, the other teams will be in there and I don't want any more trouble.

SANDRA: Don't worry about me.

BEVERLY: Look, all I'm saying is, conserve your energy.

SHENEQUA: I won't be using any energy to bust Mandy's ass at pool.

MANDY: Yeah, just watch, I'm gonna watch you bawl when you lose, you know you Africans can't tek losing your money.

MANDY and SHENEQUA walk out, followed by CARRIE who cartwheels out behind them. BEVERLY goes to her locker and takes out her purse and begins rummaging through it.

ZOWIE: I'm going out for a fag.

BEVERLY: Have you got change of a pound?

ZOWIE: Nah Bev.

ZOWIE walks out. SANDRA begins looking into her bag.

SANDRA: What do you need Bev?

BEVERLY: Just some tens for the phone.

SANDRA hands her some change

God bless you. (*She exits.*)

JACKIE: Stupid stuck up bitch! (*She takes a bottl* *locker.*) Bout drink coffee?! (*She puts bottle to h*

SANDRA: Take it easy Jack, tek time.

JACKIE: Oh for fuck sake! Not you an all, first Mandy, then Bev, and now you, look away if you can't bear it! (*She takes another swig.*)

SANDRA walks over to the chair by the window, climbs up on top of the chair and stands on tiptoes trying to look out of the window. Sound of heavy rain falling.

I can't get that fucking bitch's voice out of my head, that dirty whore was calling out his name, like he's any good. Darren! Darren! Stupid bitch! I heard it all on my mobile, that clumsy cunt, fancy him having his phone on.

SANDRA: You know how they are in the heat of the moment.

JACKIE: (*Staring at the bottle.*) I've got that fucker! (*She laughs coldly.*)

SANDRA: Suppose he denies it, you know they're all stinking rotten liars, it's not like you've got it recorded.

JACKIE: It's recorded in my head, that's all I need, that's good enough. One thing Darren can't do is lie, sorry two things, and fuck. (*She takes another swig.*)

SANDRA walks over to her, takes the bottle and puts it to her mouth and immediately starts coughing.

I hate the rain.

SANDRA: Really! I love the rain.

JACKIE: It reminds me of being stuck in the house with my Dad.

SANDRA: Your Dad was cool man, he was a laugh.

JACKIE: That was all the fucker did, he never listened, too busy bussing dry jokes and laughing at them. He'd see me crying and instead of cuddling me or suppen, he'd be laughing. 'Ah, what's all the crying about, fell off yu bike, ha ha.' I remember him coming home one evening and I was so upset, my best friend Antonia had just died, and there he was making fool fool jokes. My mum told him 'Dudley, it's Antonio,' before she could finish he had to get one in, 'what unoo had a lovers tiff, she find a new friend?' My mum told him, 'No, she's dead,' the asshole carried on laughing until it sank in, but he just stared. I saw some fluid come to his eyes, but that could've been the liquor seeping out, but I thought here comes the hug I've been waiting for, even though my friend had to die for me to get it. But the man came over and patted me on my head, like I'm a fucking dog, mumbling some shit bout time is the master. He was right, look at him now wheelchair bound. (*Slight pause.*) It's his wickedness, that's what put him there, and look who's picking up the pieces, my mother. I remember going over to Mum's, and she had popped out and left him. When I went in, he'd fallen out of the wheelchair. I just stared at him, thinking how agile he was when he used to jumpkick my mum, and now he's this frail helpless little man.

SANDRA: I would've swapped my dad for yours them days, bwoy, mine was so miserable.

JACKIE: Your Dad was scary, we used to toss a coin for who should knock your door. None of us wanted to knock it, he just looked so stern, we'd wanna run, and the house was always in darkness even in daylight.

SANDRA: Yeah that was his way of saving money, use a torch, we had to do our homework in candlelight. The only times I remember him having the living room light on was when it was Jamaica independence or when Mummy gave him a little pum pum. And that stinking paraffin heater! If he was alive today he'd still use that rather than the gas fire. Weird man, he'd lock the phones, all the bloody doors in the house would be locked and he'd be walking around like a caretaker.

JACKIE: Didn't you used to tap out the numbers on the phone though?

SANDRA: Oh my God, yes! You had to have a fast finger for that. (*Doing tapping actions.*) I member phoning Mandy and I actually got it to work, but I was in so much shock I hung up.

JACKIE empties her bottle. SHENEQUA rushes in holding her crotch. She has an earpiece from one mobile to her ear. She rests her other mobile down on the bench and sprints to the toilets.

JACKIE: You get beaten Shenequa?

SHENEQUA: Mandy got lucky, but I'm going back for my money.

She exits into the toilet. BEVERLY enters the locker room.

SANDRA: Did you get through?

BEVERLY: What?

SANDRA: The phone?

BEVERLY: Oh, it's out of order.

JACKIE: Typical! Like everything in this place. (*She exits.*)

SANDRA: I better go and look after her.

BEVERLY: She should be looking after you.

SANDRA walks out after JACKIE. BEVERLY looks at her watch. She looks around the locker room anxiously, spots SHENEQUA's phone on the bench and hesitates for a moment before picking it up. She walks towards the entrance and looks out. She walks back in and begins dialling a number.

So this pussy don't sweet you anymore! What? What did you say? I said *this pussy don't sweet you anymore!* You are going to listen to me you know, what, I am listening to you… Okay, talk then…oh! You wanna cool things down, could that be because you're screwing sister Pearl? What do you mean? You're a liar! I've heard all the gossip, how can you say that, all I did was love you, I still love you, you know that… I do love you, I do! Oh really, well I'm sorry it's not convenient for you to talk right now, but I want to talk now! You don't wanna do that you know…well maybe I should talk to your wife. (*She hangs phone up and continues talking.*) I bet she'd like to hear how you make me dress up like a public school boy, what's that about, pervert!

The shower room door opens and SHENEQUA enters, earpiece still attached. BEVERLY is in shock.

Shenequa! You're here.

She throws the phone in shock and SHENEQUA jumps and catches it.

SHENEQUA: Ole on! What you doing wit my phone?

The phone rings.

BEVERLY looks at the phone in SHENEQUA's hand. SHENEQUA is looking at BEVERLY and then looks at the phone and studies the number, puzzled.

Hertz…

She holds the phone away from her ear. We hear shouting coming from phone.

Who you calling a fucking whore? Who is this? Listen you must have the wrong number star, who? Oh Beverly, hold on. Who shall I say is calling?

SHENEQUA walks over to BEVERLY and hands her the phone.

BEVERLY: I'm not blackmailing you…when…well why can't it be tonight? Alright then, are you gonna come around? Well why can't you come to my house? I don't wanna meet on street, so what's the point in meeting to talk if you can only give me ten minutes, well there's no point is there? Look you're fucking with my head you know…fuck the language! Don't you dare! Look, I am a Christian! And you're the Minister remember, how much of those lonely single woman in that church have you *saved* already? Well I'll tell you something, this is one Christian that won't be turning the other cheek, I know how to deal with you. It's not a threat…look you know I don't mean this, I'm just upset, why you hurting me like this? Look how about I steam a nice piece of fish for y…hello, hello…

SHENEQUA: It's a bad reception in here you know, Bev.

Silence.

So what, him blow you out?

BEVERLY looks up at SHENEQUA.

Look Bev, it don't mek sense you lose your mind over any man, you see me, me have six man, all of them know about each other, I don't have no secrets and I ain't hurting no one. I just live life to the full, and I tell you suppen else, I'm well looked after.

BEVERLY: I'm not young anymore Shenequa, I'm tired, I'm tired of always getting it wrong. I try so hard, I always aim to do the right things, but somehow I always end up with nothing, no man, no kids, no family, and no friends. You lot aren't my friends, none of you like me, I know that, but that's about me and not being very likable. I've never been liked, even my mother hates me… I'll have to leave the church, where will I go? The church is suppose to be the last stop. If I fail at the church where else is there to go? Maybe I should go back to my friend Smirnoff, two bottles a day took all my problems away.

SHENEQUA: Did it though, you just couldn't remember them Bev, you said yourself this is the happiest you've ever been.

BEVERLY: Yeah well what I say and how I feel are two different things.

SHENEQUA: How do you feel now?

BEVERLY: Alone.

SHENEQUA: Do you love him more than Christ?

Silence. Crackling sound of TANNOY. Blackout.

TANNOY: Time out!

Whistle blows off stage. Lights up. Very tight spot on BEVERLY's face.

BEVERLY: Dear Lord, please forgive me, though I know just what I've done, I've sinned, Jesus! The sex was good though, so why should I feel guilty? How can I possibly put a foot in that church again? Life is a bitch, boy, you make all the changes to suit them and then what, they change on you. 'Reserve your place in heaven,' was the beautiful words written on the card that Minister Brown gave to me. Lord! What he must've thought when he saw me, especially when the Vodka bottles rolled out of my bag, but, everything for a reason, because out of bad came good, that was the last time I touched alcohol. Who would've thought, Beverly Ordene Scott, a Christian, and here I go again messing up, through man… I don't even know if I love him! The only man I can say I loved was John, wow, he helped me to find my roots, but even with all the flowers, the holidays, the gifts, oh and that beautiful proposal he made to me over the karaoke machine, we were so pissed! But you still can't put all your eggs into one bowl, I mean as soon as a problem arises it's crash bang! All over. I lost my womb and then I lost John. But hey! That's life, from John to Smirnoff to Minister Brown. 'As I walk through the valley of the shadow of death' as he sexed out my soul, I was overwhelmed, and all I could say was: 'Fuck me! Minister Brown! Fuck me Minister Brown!' 'I will fear no evil for thou art with me thy rod and thy staff will comfort me.'

Whistle blows off stage. Fade to black. Lights up on locker room. ZOWIE enters.

ZOWIE: I think you should go and have a word with Jackie, you know Bev, she's lean up on the bar.

SHENEQUA: I ain't playing with that bloody drunk again you know, you better go and talk to her cos I don't want to open my mouth.

ZOWIE: You alright Bev? You been crying? You look a bit spaced out.

SHENEQUA: Yeah netball pressures!

Sound of thunder and lightening clapping. The lights flicker on and off before going out completely.

(*She lights a lighter.*) I don't like the dark.

BEVERLY: The Gods are angry.

Blackout.

Scene 3

We come up on the ladies all sitting around in the locker room; the power is still out and they are in darkness except for a few candles. We hear the rain falling and thunder rumbling. There is a bucket stage left catching the drips of water from the leaking roof. There is a subdued atmosphere. BEVERLY is sitting on a bench reading her bible and mumbling to herself, SANDRA is biting her nails looking into space, SHENEQUA is playing a computer game on her mobile, CARRIE is writing in her diary looking very happy and ZOWIE is reading the Black Hair and Beauty magazine. She has a pen to her mouth and is occasionally sipping from a can of coke. JACKIE is trying to glue her phone back together but to no avail and MANDY has her headphones on from her walkman. Her eyes are closed as she rocks to the music. Mandy begins drumming a beat on her lap. The beat falls in tune with the sound of the dripping water. CARRIE joins in beating out another rhythm on her diary and a beautiful sound begins to emerge. JACKIE starts a rhythm slapping her hands on the floor, BEVERLY starts to clap her hands, SANDRA stomps her feet and claps her hands and ZOWIE taps the coke tin with her pen. MANDY becomes aware of everyone joining in with her beat and removes her headphones. SHENEQUA uses the rings on her mobile to join in. The sound is 'wicked' and everyone chants 'boom!'. The rhythm keeps building. MANDY feels a vibe and starts to hum a beautiful haunting melody: 'No Woman No Cry'. SHENEQUA is winding her waist seductively to the beat, MANDY begins to sing out and everyone is totally lost in the moment. It builds and builds until we hear the playing of an out of tune recorder. CARRIE is doing ballet moves while playing the recorder. Everyone starts laughing and jeering and the rhythm disintegrates.

BEVERLY: That voice is a gift Mandy.

MANDY: Thanks.

CARRIE: You should be in musicals, you could be the next Elaine Paige.

JACKIE: I can't picture Mandy in *Cats*.

CARRIE: Maybe not *Cats*, but what about *Starlight Express*, all that skating, what fun!

MANDY: When you ever see me skate?

CARRIE: Everyone skates, uh! Don't tell me you can't skate!

Tthe lights flicker back on.

SHENEQUA: Thank fuck for that, that fool caretaker actually got it working.

ZOWIE: Sing us another song, Mand.

MANDY: Wait, you think me is a juke box, I sing when the vibe takes me, and right now is a spliff vibe me on.

SHENEQUA: I'm proper bored man.

Her phone rings.

Saved by the bell. (*She starts mumbling into her phone.*)

JACKIE: Do you know what this reminds me of?

MANDY: What?

JACKIE: Do you remember that time the coach broke down when we were on our way to play that match against The She Devils in Liverpool?

SANDRA: Do I? We were on that coach for over two hours, we couldn't even stretch our legs cos it was pissing down.

CARRIE: What an adventure that was.

SHENEQUA: Breaking down on the M25 is not my idea of an adventure, that's a proper nightmare.

BEVERLY: I praised God when we broke down, I thought that man was going to kill us, he couldn't drive.

MANDY: He was too tired to drive, he was sleeping on the motorway, Shenequa had to poke him twice to wake him up.

BEVERLY: Yeah, I had to send Carrie up front to sit with him and she started to play her recorder, that woke him up.

ZOWIE: That's when he really put his foot down.

SANDRA: We should've known the man was dodgy, especially after he told us how many cars he'd written off.

SHENEQUA: Yeah look how his face was all choppy choppy.

ZOWIE: What was funny, was when he heard the police sirens, he flew off that bloody coach and ran off down the motorway like a man possessed.

They all laugh.

CARRIE: And he forgot to put his shoes on.

BEVERLY: Course he'd forget to put his shoes on, the man had no tax, no insurance, no license and he's driving a stolen coach, he must run.

SHENEQUA: Yeah, run off with me ten pound for the draw I sell him.

SANDRA: No wonder the man couldn't stay awake.

SHENEQUA: Yeah boy, macca draw that.

MANDY: Bev? What did you say to those coppers? Cos all I remember is you coming on the coach and telling us to grab our things and get into the meat wagon.

ZOWIE: We arrived in style though, innit?

JACKIE: The look on the She Devil's faces when they saw us pouring out of the Police van.

SHENEQUA: We looked like proper convicts man.

ZOWIE: That was a wicked game wasn't it?

MANDY: The minute that whistle blew, I knew the game was ours, everything just felt right.

SHENEQUA: They were fighting for a feel of the ball!

MANDY: I caught the ball from Sandra, one two, and then I pivot around to Jackie.

JACKIE: I'm ready for that ball, I catch the ball, looking at the net, can't see a way in, I pass to Carrie

CARRIE: I got the ball from Jackie, I make a move to shoot, fake her out and dodge to the left and pass to Shenequa.

BEVERLY: They were all over you at that point.

SHENEQUA: I never watch that, I done a few turns on them, my girl got dizzy, one two pass her and shot!

They all act out their moves.

ZOWIE: That was a classy move that.

SANDRA: We played zone for that match didn't we?

JACKIE: That was the last time we brought home a cup.

MANDY: What happened to that cup?

BEVERLY: Don't mention that.

ZOWIE: Didn't we leave it in that club with no name.

SANDRA: They wouldn't let us back in to get it.

CARRIE: Why were we thrown out again?

SHENEQUA: Noh Bev! She was giving the owner's husband a lap dance in his wheelchair, the man couldn't get her off, by the time the bouncers came over, Bev start cussing some dutty words, and we were asked to leave.

BEVERLY: I'm sure someone spiked my drinks. Well thank God I don't drink anymore, I don't need it.

SANDRA: We've had some times man. I think I was happy then, Mum was still alive.

JACKIE: I was nice and slim then.

SANDRA: I've never been slim, Mum was slim. I think I take after Dad, which is not so bad, he was a bit cranky, but his heart was in the right place, it's a pity Scooty's wasn't.

BEVERLY: Let us not dwell on that Sandra, for the Lord says, 'when mine enemies are turned back, they shall fall and perish at thy presence.'

ZOWIE goes to the toilet.

ZOWIE: (*Puts her head around the door.*) The bulb's blown, it's dark in here, as anyone got a spare light bulb?

SHENEQUA: (*Opens her legs.*) See one ya.

ZOWIE exits into toilet.

CARRIE: I've got some light bulbs.

CARRIE gets up and goes over to her locker and takes out the wedding gift that SANDRA had given back to her. She begins to unwrap the gift to reveal a box of light bulbs.

SHENEQUA: What! You buy the girl pure light bulbs for her wedding gift?

CARRIE: I thought it was a good idea.

JACKIE: Why?

CARRIE: Because her house is always in darkness.

SHENEQUA: That's long man.

CARRIE: I bet none of you lot would've thought of buying that, what did yous buy her.

SHENEQUA: Don't worry yuself, not a box of bulbs.

BEVERLY: It's the thought that counts.

ZOWIE comes out of the toilet and stands looking at CARRIE's gift.

ZOWIE: What's that?

SANDRA: My wedding gift.

ZOWIE: Oh, we opening gifts are we? Don't you mind, Sandra?

SANDRA: Nah, go on man.

SHENEQUA: What you get Zowie?

ZOWIE goes to her locker and everyone follows. They all take their gifts out and begin to unwrap them. ZOWIE reveals her gift first. She takes out a small box and begins opening the box. The girls are watching her. She then takes out a square box with an on off switch, three lights and a plug flex and holds it up.

JACKIE: What's that?

ZOWIE: You don't know what this is? Everyone should have one they're brilliant.

JACKIE: Yes, but what is it?

SHENEQUA: She noh know.

ZOWIE: Actually, it's an ionizer!

CARRIE: I know, it's for electric shock treatment.

ZOWIE: No Carrie, that's for mad people. This is an ionizer, it purifies the air, and therefore produces a sense of well being.

SHENEQUA: Some middle class crap the best air is fresh air.

SANDRA: Oh my God! Mandy, where did you get that from? (*She picks the CD up.*) This has been deleted, do you know how long I've searched for this one?

MANDY: I know, I had to order it, take it man.

SANDRA: I think I will.

SHENEQUA: Not Frankie bloody Sinatra! I thought you had them all by now.

SANDRA: Not this one, put it on Mand.

MANDY takes the CD and puts it into the CD player. The song plays low in the background. JACKIE unwraps her present to reveal a beautiful carving of a black man and woman embracing.

ZOWIE: Cor, that's beautiful! How much did that set you back?

SHENEQUA: You don't ask big people that.

MANDY: Where did you get that from?

JACKIE: From Rolo's.

BEVERLY: Rolo? I thought he sells food.

ZOWIE: Yeah wicked patties.

SHENEQUA: You know how them black man stay, them have a food shop, and them sell everything from fry fish to a three piece suite.

MANDY: That's right I bought a leather jacket from him.

JACKIE: Well he's selling these for an African man he met in Brixton, reckon's the guy's a king.

MANDY: Show me a African man who isn't a king.

SHENEQUA: Well at least they have a aim and a goal, an at…

JACKIE: (*Cuts in.*) Anyway as I was saying, it has special meanings, apparently, it's suppose to bring you good fortune.

SHENEQUA: Well in that case, that should've been a pre-wedding gift. (*Laughs aloud, alone.*)

CARRIE holds the carving and examines it.

CARRIE: What does this mean? Onea meeny ura woo.

SHENEQUA takes the carving from CARRIE.

SHENEQUA: Onyami nhyira wo…may your path be rocky.

CARRIE: Aahh.

ZOWIE: Charming.

SHENEQUA: It's Twi.

CARRIE: It weren't bad.

SHENEQUA: It's an African language, stupid!

JACKIE: That's the first time I've heard you speak African, you always chat like a yardie.

SHENEQUA: That's because that's all you lot understand. I actually speak six languages, Twi, Yoruba, Ewe, Kokuyu, English and yard style.

JACKIE: We call it broken English dear.

CARRIE: Speak African for us, go on.

SHENEQUA: There are over two hundred different languages in Africa, it's a massive continent you know, and I only speak four of them, which one you want?

MANDY: Gwan Shenequa!

CARRIE: I wish I could speak another language.

SHENEQUA: You used to, you just lost it man, that's why you lot are bitter.

JACKIE: I'm doing just fine with my English, I ain't bitter cos I can't speak bloody African.

SHENEQUA: Why should you be, you're an African woman who can't speak her own language.

CARRIE: Am I African?

SHENEQUA: You're all African! Even Zowie.

CARRIE: Is she? She hasn't got the classic African nose, her nose is far too straight.

MANDY: Well the Somalians has straight noses, and they're Africans.

CARRIE: I don't actually feel African.

BEVERLY: Neither do I, I feel more English.

SHENEQUA: I rest my case, divided we fall.

MANDY: Well history has definitely proved that one.

SHENEQUA begins to unwrap her present to reveal a big black dildo.

SANDRA: History has proved that man is evil and will always be.

SHENEQUA: See evil ya. (*She holds up the dildo.*)

SHENEQUA switches it on and the dildo begins to vibrate.

CARRIE: Oh my God! Can I have that?

ZOWIE: That's not a very romantic wedding gift.

SHENEQUA: Trust me, man love to see a woman use a dildo, it send them wild.

JACKIE: You are one kinky little girl.

CARRIE: Are you into bondage?

SHENEQUA: How you mean! Me love tying up a man.

JACKIE: Do you let them tie you up too?

SHENEQUA: Only if I really like them.

MANDY: Have you ever tried the hot wax?

SHENEQUA: Oh yeah baby.

CARRIE: What's that?

SHENEQUA: Goh buy a book man.

JACKIE: I've always dreamed about wild hot nasty kinky sex.

BEVERLY: Well, it's out there.

JACKIE: How do you know?

BEVERLY: Because I'm out there, but just be careful what you wish for.

SANDRA: Yeah cos it never comes true.

SHENEQUA: All I know is I have to get my tings good, and my man must be able to stan pon it long, you gets me.

MANDY: I'm coming back as a man with a big cock.

ZOWIE: Size doesn't matter.

BEVERLY: Yes it does!

MANDY: Eh eh, yu dat Bev.

JACKIE: Well if I was coming back as a man, I'd definitely want a big cock.

ZOWIE: To do what with?

JACKIE: To fuck them and show them what it's like.

SANDRA: I'd never want to be a man, they're too weak.

BEVERLY: Too selfish.

JACKIE: Too greedy.

ZOWIE: Lazy.

CARRIE: Happy!

TANNOY kicks in.

TANNOY: We have an urgent call for Mandy Bliss, could Mandy Bliss please report to the caretaker's office, you have an urgent call.

MANDY looks alarmed.

MANDY: Jesus Christ! (*She runs out of the room.*)

ZOWIE: I hope Cora's alright.

CARRIE walks over to the window and climbs on the chair. They are all concerned.

CARRIE: It's stopped raining!

The girls cheer.

JACKIE: (*Stretching.*) I'm getting stiff man.

ZOWIE: Well I'm ready for the Ziggy Lights.

CARRIE: I can't believe we're playing them, I wont be making any mistakes in this game.

SHENEQUA: That would make a nice change.

BEVERLY is looking at herself in the mirror. MANDY runs on, out of breath.

MANDY: Sandra.

SANDRA: What?

MANDY: Sandra, I just had your brother on the phone. Sandra, the police are at your house.

SANDRA: Have they found him?

MANDY: What happened, Sandra?

SANDRA: I killed Scooty.

SHENEQUA: Bloodclaut!

SANDRA: I think he died after the first stab, well he stopped moving. I just kept stabbing him, I couldn't stop. He came to collect his clothes. I begged him to hold me, so he took me to bed. He said I was a good girl but he had to go, so, I picked up the bread knife and pushed it into his heart. He stared wide-eyed at me for a long time trying to speak. I wish I knew what the fucker wanted to say. I'm going to jail.

CARRIE: You can't go to jail, just run Sandra.

SHENEQUA: You can't tell her that, you'll be an accessory to the crime, that carries at least a five year sentence, bwoy. This is some heavy duty shit.

BEVERLY: You must pray for forgiveness, get down on your knees and beg for forgiveness. (*She goes down on her knees.*) Blessed is he whose transgression is forgiven, whose sin is covered.

SANDRA: I'm not sorry, Bev, he got what he deserved. I'm happy to do time for him. He broke my heart and I'll never be able to mend that.

JACKIE walks over and holds SANDRA. After a while SANDRA pulls away.

SANDRA: I'm alright, I'm not even scared, it was the right thing to do, he had to pay.

Sound of TANNOY kicking in.

TANNOY: Will the Ziggy Lights and the V.I.P. Crew please report to court three to commence play?

BEVERLY: I suppose I better let them know we're pulling from this game.

SANDRA: I came here to play Bev, I say we play.

ZOWIE: I don't know if I can.

JACKIE: We can't play now, Sandra, it's, it's… I don't know, it's, look I don't think it's right.

MANDY: It's too dark, man.

BEVERLY: We must show some respect for the dead, the Lord says…

SANDRA is stretching and doing warm up moves. CARRIE joins her.

SHENEQUA: The Lord says an eye for an eye, the debt is settled.

BEVERLY: Except in the eyes of the Lord.

JACKIE: I'm in shock, Sandra who wouldn't kill a spider.

CARRIE goes into the splits.

CARRIE: It's a crime of passion.

BEVERLY: Sandra, please stop doing that, there's no need to warm up, we can't play, I'm sorry.

SANDRA: I'm playing.

She walks over and picks up a netball.

JACKIE: You're still in shock Sandra, you're not thinking straight.

SANDRA bounces the ball.

SANDRA: What's new, I want this game.

TANNOY: Will the V.I.P. Crew please report to court three immediately.

SANDRA holds the ball in the air.

SANDRA: Who wants it?

SHENEQUA: (*Holds her hands up.*) I'll have some.

SANDRA throws the ball to SHENEQUA.

BEVERLY: Look! Stop this!

BEVERLY tries to take the ball from SHENEQUA but she defends the ball. ZOWIE goes to her locker and begins to take her bags out.

SHENEQUA: Where you going?

ZOWIE: I'm going home.

SHENEQUA: What the fuck is this none of us even liked him, me nah grieve fe him, the guy was shoddy, him dead and we can't bring him back.

MANDY: The Police are on their way here, Shenequa.

SHENEQUA: Well we better hurry up then, this is our time to shine, this is our netball moment, why the fuck do we gather in a damp locker room on a rainy Saturday? Because we love netball, no point pretending not to for fear of losing, we are all good enough to win. We've been given another chance to shine it don't matter if things go wrong dread, we have to be wrong and strong, don't be dwelling on mistakes, because while we're stressing the other team will be scoring. The key word for this game is *forward!* I think we should play zone defence on this game, what do you think, Bev? If we defend as a team they wont be able to break the zone. They're gonna get frustrated and tired.

BEVERLY walks over to SHENEQUA and puts her fist out. BEVERLY touches her fist and MANDY touches SANDRA's fist. All the girls touch fists. MANDY takes off her Goal Attack bib and hands it to SANDRA who removes the Goal Keeper bib and hands it to MANDY and puts the Goal Attack bib on.

BEVERLY: Let us jog to victory, ladies.

We hear Frank Sinatra singing 'The Best is Yet to Come'.
They all jog out. SANDRA is last. She looks around and jogs
out. A slow fade on the locker room.

The End.